WOMEN IN VENTURE CAPITAL

WOMEN IN VENTURE CAPITAL

HOW TO BREAK INTO THE BOYS
CLUB OF VENTURE CAPITAL:
LESSONS LEARNED FROM
THE BEST OF THE BEST

KARINA CHAN

NEW DEGREE PRESS

WOMEN IN VENTURE CAPITAL

How to Break into the Boys Club of Venture Capital: Lessons Learned from the Best of the Best

ISBN   978-1-64137-153-7   *Paperback*

          978-1-64137-154-4   *Ebook*

To my father and his jovial humor.

To my brother and his never-ending ambition.

To my mother and her elegant tenacity.

CONTENTS

INTRODUCTION   9

PART 1.   **HOW WE GOT HERE**   **23**
CHAPTER 1.   UNPACKING THE "PIPELINE" PROBLEM   25
CHAPTER 2.   THE ELEPHANT IN THE VALLEY   33
CHAPTER 3.   GETTING OFF THE FLOOR... LITERALLY.   49

PART 2.   **WHAT WE'RE DOING**   **61**
CHAPTER 4.   IT'S IN THE DETAILS.   63
CHAPTER 5.   GET NERDY, GO DEEP   75
CHAPTER 6.   KNOW YOUR PRODUCT   83
CHAPTER 7.   BE AN INDUSTRY SPECIALIST   93

PART 3.   **WHERE WE'RE GOING**   **113**
CHAPTER 8.   SUPPORTING FEMALE INVESTORS ALSO
                MEANS SUPPORTING FEMALE FOUNDERS.   115
CHAPTER 9.   RETHINK IMPACT, RETHINK INVESTING   125
CHAPTER 10. BEYOND VENTURE CAPITAL   137
                CONCLUSION   151
                ACKNOWLEDGEMENTS   157
                APPENDIX   159

INTRODUCTION

———

It happens all the time when my husband and I are at work events together. Cocktail Party Guy asks my husband about how things are going at his news site, and he answers. Then Cocktail Party Guy asks me how our dogs are, and I answer, before pivoting the conversation back to work—and later rolling my eyes as we walk away. It is not impolite. It is not inappropriate. But it is still, at least in my mind, sexist. Both my husband and I love our work. Both my husband and I husband love our dogs. One of us gets asked about our work. One of us gets asked about our dogs.

It is a form of soft discrimination that I fear might be all too familiar to all too many women, and often I find it hard to explain to my male friends and colleagues. Occasionally, I even find myself struggling to convince them that it is discrimination, and that it has consequences.

I found myself going back to those moments with Cocktail Party Guy while following Ellen Pao's lawsuit against her former employer, the powerhouse venture capital firm Kleiner, Perkins, Caufield and Byers. In the suit, Pao argued that the firm failed to promote her because of her gender. But it was not a cut-and-dry case. Much of it centered around those Cocktail Party Guy moments, ones where one reasonable observer might see nothing going on and another reasonable observer might see clear evidence of sexism.

-- ANNIE LOWREY, *THE NEW YORK MAGAZINE, MARCH 30, 2015*[1]

Ellen Pao wasn't the first woman (or man) to point out the unfortunate consequences of the boys' club that is venture capital.

But she was one of the loudest, especially given that her claims were made against one of the blue-bloods of the venture capital ecosystem Kleiner Perkins.

Pao really shouldn't have had to say anything. The numbers pretty much tell the story.

Seven percent of partners at the top one hundred venture firms are women.

---

1 Lowrey, Annie. 2018. "Ellen Pao And The Sexism You Can't Quite Prove". *Intelligencer.*

I'm not here to throw stones at the industry. That's been done and in many ways the data speaks for itself.

Instead this book is written to showcase hope for what's ahead.

* * *

All my outside activities, extracurricular readings, and my required off-campus events led me to the same conclusion. As progressive and modern as entrepreneurship and venture capital are supposed to be, both industries lack the diverse body of employees to show for it.

My curiosity on this topic was first piqued while I was competing on an all-male team at the Undergraduate Venture Capital Investment Competition. It was only a five-person team, so I figured there's no way the gender dynamics would even matter on such a small scale. It is a freaking college simulation of an investment. How much could it get into people's heads? Plus, I liked all the guys in my team. They seemed like a smart and capable group.

As soon as we got the pitch decks from the company, though, it was like an unnecessarily aggressive alter-ego came out of everybody.

"Dude, what the hell is this pitch deck?"

"I don't know, man, but we don't actually have to fucking invest in them. We just have to find the fund fit and throw, like, three million at them and be done with it."

Everyone became louder, more opinionated, sassier, and we were all interrupting each other. It wasn't because we didn't like each other. Suddenly when you put $100M of fake money in the hands of insecure college students (including me), they get so much cockier.

There was a dramatic increase in the amount of swearing but not at anyone or anything. Was a four-letter word here or there going to add any more value to this discussion on this company's valuation? No. But the effect it did have was to establish a sense of dominance and aggressiveness to "venture capital bros" (think Ed Chen from HBO's Silicon Valley) that really didn't need to be there to get a deal done.

I am a very straightforward person. If I think an idea is stupid, I will say so, but I don't need to talk over other people to get my point across or add swear words here or there to validate what I'm saying. I get it. The dollar amounts are large and the risks are high. Everyone is stressed to the max. It is understandable that emotions can be all over the place. Yet, if I wanted to be a contributive VC team member, I had to talk just as loudly, just as confidently (even though none of us knew what we were doing), and swear just as much.

Otherwise, my thoughts probably wouldn't have been heard. I would have been drowned out and I've still never been mansplained over so much before so much in my life.

Someone asked why the difference between a pre-money valuation and post-money valuation mattered and I would explain, "Isn't it significant because if you invest a portion of your money into two companies, one at a million in post-money and one at a million in pre-money, your investment in the post-money company elicits a higher ownership stake because the valuation includes your investment within it?"

One of my team members looked me in the eye and said, " Oh, Karina, I can explain it. It is like if you invest the same amount of money into a pre- and post-money company with the same valuation, you'd get a bigger portion of the post-money company."

Let me be straight.

I don't think my teammates are bad people.

I've become really close friends with two of my teammates since UVCIC (including the one that mansplained all over me at the time).

I don't think it is them.

But there seems to be something about venture capital that brings out this "bro"liness in people. People feel they have to become this trope of the venture capitalist in order to be successful, and that expectation is 92 percent male.

After some initial digging, I found the numbers for female representation in venture capital to be downright appalling. According to Crunchbase, in 2017, only 8 percent of investment-making roles at top companies were held by women. PitchBook also reports that in 2017 only 2 percent of all venture capital dollars went to women.[2]

After interviewing Leslie Jump from Startup Angels, I learned that the numbers are much more favorable to women when it comes to micro-VCs or women who have started their own fund, but not much data is collected for that metric. According to Crunchbase, in the last three years, women have funded sixteen micro-VC funds ($50 Million fund size or under) which make up 21 percent of all the funds in that space.[3] In fact, the only well-known statistics on the topic are very few and come from PitchBook or Crunchbase. Furthermore, there is no data at all for non-gender-binary conforming people in investing roles.

2   Zarya, Valentina. 2018. "Female Founders Got 2% of Venture Capital Dollars in 2017". *Fortune.*

3   Teare, Genè, and Ned Desmond. 2018. "Announcing The 2017 Update To The Crunchbase Women In Venture Report". *Techcrunch.*

I was surprised that while interviewing women, I found so many possible reasons for the gender disparity in venture capital that wasn't what I'd already found in articles online. The issue is a lot more nuanced than one would imagine. First of all, given the power structure of venture capital firms, it is not meaningful to have many female junior staffers and executive assistants but no women in roles that actually get to sign off on a check. Thus, the metric we must look for is not the overall composition of women in a firm, but the number of women in general partner or managing partner roles. When looking for female general partners to interview through LinkedIn searches, I found many women with the VC firm name in their titles, but only a handful with investing roles. I found one woman with the title "General Partner" every five or seven pages of search results. If women are only confined to secretarial roles or kept as token members in junior classes, that perpetuates the idea that women are not good enough to handle the fundamental, value-added part of a business.

* * *

This book is built upon the lives and lessons of the women in venture deals, the ones who can pave the way by teaching other young women how to claim a stake in this space. From these doyennes, the venture capital community and the reader will learn how to consider the iconic Sand Hill to be Sandy's hill too.

For the past year, I set out on a quest to find hope and answers to the gender issues everyone seems to recognize in the world of venture capital.

My mission:

- Discover why this characteristically male phenomenon exists in venture capital.
- Illustrate, through the few and the talented who have made it into that sliver of positions, how a woman in school like me can carve a path to also work in one of the coolest jobs.
- Learn the nuances of what you may face in this industry and learn from the crème de la crème about how to hop over these obstacles.

This book is meant for any woman (though non-gender-binary conforming partners are next to nonexistent but that's a whole other book) thinking about entering this boys' club industry.

And at its' core, it is a book about the women who are already making a difference… and how the rest of us can follow their lead. Venture capital is a meaningful industry, which women should feel confident in pursuing and men should encourage.

A PRIMER ON VENTURE CAPITAL

So... We've heard of venture capital before. Otherwise, we wouldn't be reading this book. However, not all of us are experts in venture capital yet. Perhaps you're here because you've heard venture capital has had a hand in creating the biggest companies in the world. In order to understand how power dynamics and gender dynamics work within a Venture Capital fund, an understanding of the different roles within a fund and how funds function is imperative. Since this is meant to be written to an audience of college-age women like me, I've written this chapter for those of you who are new to the inner workings of venture capital. If you're already an expert, go along to read the fascinating stories of incredible, representative partners.

This is not an in-depth explanation of the venture capital structure, but was written to help contextualize the stories of the women mentioned in this book. This diagram is a pretty comprehensive visual representation of how a venture capital firm is structured:

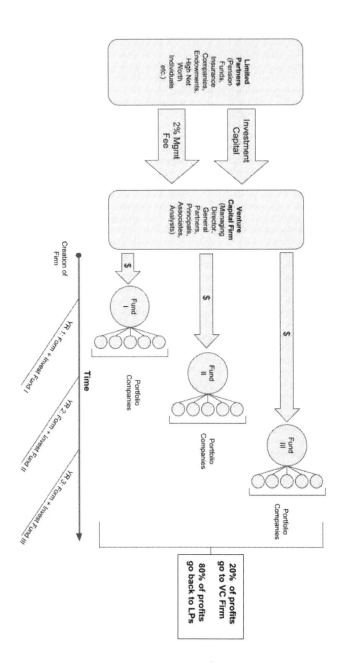

Much like how startups pitch to venture capital investors for funding, the investors themselves pitch to **limited partners** for funding as well. Limiter partners are pension funds, insurance companies, endowments and other establishments that give capital to the VC firm whenever they raise money for funds. The venture capital firm takes a 2% management fee that becomes fixed annual income for the members of the firm. The rest of that money gets distributed into the **fund**.

The fund's goal is to make a return the fund, and some more, to its LPs. Funds distribute investments into several **portfolio companies**. The fund will invest money into a portfolio company proportionately with its valuation so that it can retain a certain percentage ownership of that company. Let's illustrate this with a very simplified example. Say a firm receives $15M from its limited partners to create a fund. Say the fund invests $15M in company A and that investment brings the valuation of the company to $100M. Now the fund has a 15% ownership stake of company A. Portfolio companies take the capital from VCs and use it to operate and grow their business, further increasing their worth and valuation. What funds are looking for are **exits**, liquidity events where the fund can realize their return on their investment. Exits can be Initial Public Offerings (IPOs) or acquisitions by larger companies. When the company goes public or the company gets bought, the VC is paid their ownership stake based off the current valuation.

Let's simulate a very basic example of an exit. Say company A has grown its business for a few years and is about to be bought out at a valuation of $500M by some larger company. The VC gets 15% of the $500M or $75M in return. They've returned their $15M fund and made $60M of profit or **carried interest**. 20% of the carry goes back to the VC as a commission of sorts, and the other 80% goes back to the limited partners.

Please note that outside this example and in reality, a fund would never ever invest all its money into one startup as that is an incredibly risky decision. VC funds will spread out their investments over several companies to minimize risk. The above example is just to show how money flows from the LP to the VC to its investments and back around. A VC is cyclically raising money for funds, deploying capital, and (hopefully) collecting returns. A VC firm has several funds, each of which have a five to ten-year lifespan. There is a plethora of other factors that come with venture investments: board seats, syndicating and more but those are all things that I urge the reader to study on their own time. I learned what I currently know from an informative book called *Venture Deals* by Brad Feld.[4]

Within a VC firm are managing and general partners, principals, associates, and analysts (in descending order within the

4 Feld, Brad, and Jason Mendelson. 2016. *Venture Deals*. Hoboken, NJ: Wiley.

hierarchy). Managing and general partners have the ability to guide the fund, write the check to invest in a company and are the most senior people in the fund. Principals and associates help bring startups into the fund and guide them through the funding process while analysts do much of the due diligence and research. We will be focusing on women who are at the partner level in this book—women who can make the investment—as this is the most impactful role in a VC yet is also the role with the least women.

PART I

HOW WE GOT HERE

CHAPTER 1

UNPACKING THE "PIPELINE" PROBLEM

———

A lot of venture capital investors like to call the lack of women getting venture capital jobs the "pipeline problem." This is what the average believer of the "pipeline problem" would say:

"I think the issue begins in our high schools, and where women particularly in America and also in Europe, tend to elect not to study the sciences when they're 11 or 12. So suddenly the hiring pool is much smaller. In fact, we just hired a young woman from Stanford who is every bit as good as her peers. And if there are more like her, we'll hire them. What we're not prepared to do is to lower our standards."[5]

5   Kulwin, Noah. 2018. "Venerated VC Michael Moritz Opens Mouth, Inserts Foot On Question About Hiring Women". *Recode.*

Whoa, whoa, whoa. First of all, Michael Moritz, it is ridiculous to say that if people don't know they're going to be a scientist by the time they're eleven or twelve, they're automatically unqualified to become a venture capital investor. This is a very odd statement coming from the Sequoia Capital Chairman who studied history. Clearly, that requirement isn't met by all male VCs either, so why is that a determining factor for females?

Second, saying you're not ready to "lower your standards" by hiring women insinuates there are not enough women who want these roles and also not enough qualified women to take them. Both of which are not true. They're out there. You just never bothered to look. I took a look instead and wrote this book to 1) prove that qualified and passionate women in venture capital exist, 2) compile their lessons learned to show young women interested in venture capital how to pursue this career path, and 3) explore the idea that ratio of women to men in venture capital is even more disproportionate than that those who study the sciences. According to the US Department of Commerce: "While nearly as many women hold undergraduate degrees as men overall, they make up only about 30 percent of all STEM degree holders."[6] Yet according to Crunchbase, females hold 8 percent of partner roles at the largest venture firms, and women hold 15 percent

6 "Women In STEM: 2017 Update". 2018. *Department Of Commerce.*

of the partner roles at accelerators and corporate venture firms.[7]

The "pipeline problem" isn't a real explanation at all. Rather it is a flimsy Band-Aid, doing a poor job of covering the gushing wound we know as extreme gender inequality reflected in venture capital.

Many of the female VCs I've talked to also agree that the real problem does not take the shape of the "pipeline problem." First of all, press around gender equality in venture capital is almost always negative. Even if you had an interest and passion for a field, could you remain unperturbed by the fact that the odds are against you to begin with? There are so few women in venture capital to begin with that you're unlikely to come across someone you feel comfortable approaching to be able to talk about the industry. As a woman, though you may have a potential interest in the field, you are less likely to know about it because you probably won't have a network that expands into the realm of venture capital. It is much more likely a guy would know another guy who works at X firm than it is for a woman to say she knows another woman who works at X venture capital firm. Your network as a woman in venture capital, one

---

7   "Women In Science, Technology, Engineering, And Mathematics (STEM)". 2018. *Catalyst*.

of the most network-driven businesses, is already smaller to begin with.

The tendency to network and make friends with people of the same gender is a known scientific process known as homophily.

A 2002 study done by sociology researchers at the University of California Irvine studied groups of men and women and tracked census data to identify patterns in the way the sexes network in "Social Networks and Job Search Outcomes Among Male and Female Professional, Technical, and Managerial Workers," published in *Sociological Focus*.

Torres and Matt L. Huffman, the authors of the study, discovered that men and women tend to build networks comprising of people in their own gender. However, women tend to recognize the disparity and attempt to fix it. Women's networks average to about 50 percent men. However, men's networks include very few women.[8]

Second, venture capital is not an industry that actively recruits. If you're in college like me, you've probably seen companies come to your campus for recruitment events to

8   Torres, Lisa, and Matt L. Huffman. 2002. "Social Networks And Job Search Outcomes Among Male And Female Professional, Technical, And Managerial Workers". Sociological Focus 35 (1): 25-42. doi:10.10 80/00380237.2002.10571218.

build relationships with potential hires and guide candidates through the application process. Venture capital firms don't do that. Andreessen Horowitz doesn't have a "Now Hiring!" sign.

Venture capital is an exclusive club that only grows through a non-systematic yet very selective process. That selectiveness comes from already knowing the people who already work there. Not only must you know them, but they must have had enough working experience with you in the past to vet your value for the company. The employee must believe you have some value-add, you are legitimate, and you have a good way of analyzing the potential growth of companies.

Since there is only a 2 percent management fee in a fund,[9] there isn't enough money or human resources to conduct extensive hiring efforts. Instead of digging to find the best talent, a new hire only joins when someone on the team already knew they'd be a good fit for the firm. Venture investment has had the motto of being extremely risky, and traditional wisdom identifies the risk-taking macho male psyche. However, females are equally able to take calculated risks. Despite that fact and by nature of pattern recognition and homophily, the mostly male network of venture capital ends up hiring out of the same pool.

---

9   Bearman, Asher. 2018. "How VC Funds Work - Expenses And Management Fees | The Venture Alley". *The Venture Alley.* https://www.theventurealley.com/2011/01/how-vc-funds-work-expenses-and-management-fees/.

Columnist Kevin Fogarty from Ladder.com sums it up perfectly: "According to Torres' and Huffman's theory of social networking: Because men hold 80 percent of the jobs in senior management (a figure that has been steadily declining), they are more likely to hear about job openings at the senior-management level. Men pass the news on to their mostly male social networks, and it is likely that news about the job opening reaches women only after it has reached and passed several men."[10]

Stephanie Palmeri from Uncork Capital illustrated this very well: "I think oftentimes what happens, and this isn't unique to venture, is when you have a job description or an idea in your mind of what a partner needs to look like and you say in order to be a partner at a venture capital fund they have to check these boxes. It might be at least this much time as an operator or as a founder and they have to have investment experience. What I think happens is that a lot of times firms start out with this concept of the profile they're looking for and then they bend these rules when they find candidates they know and are familiar with through their network. And they don't bend the rules when it comes to a candidate that maybe isn't as obvious. I think that has historically been one of the challenges that presents itself many times or is referred to as a pipeline problem. I think the reality is we're willing as an

10 Fogarty, Kevin. 2018. "Why Men Have Stronger Professional Networks Than Women". *Ladders*.

industry to bend the rules for candidates who look the way we look and we know them versus other candidates. I think the bar for women and underrepresented minorities is higher."

To Moritz's last point that Sequoia hasn't hired any women because they couldn't find any women who are qualified enough in STEM fields is just false. They were not looking hard enough. In 2016, women on corporate boards (16 percent) were almost twice as likely as their male counterparts (9 percent) to have professional technology experience among 518 Forbes Global 2000 companies.[11]

Ann Miura-Ko has a BS in Electrical Engineering from Yale, and a PhD in Quantitative Modeling of Computer Security. Jenny Abramson graduated with honors on her BA and MA from Stanford, she got the Dean's Award from Harvard Business School when she nabbed her MBA, and was a Fulbright Scholar focusing on Human Genomics at The London School of Economics. Nathalie Molina Nino sold her first company at the age of twenty. There are qualified women for these positions.

How do you navigate an industry that recruits so stealthily and is more inclined to hire males? You have to stand out and outperform. If everyone goes through the door, jump

---

11 "Women In Science, Technology, Engineering, And Mathematics (STEM)". 2018. *Catalyst.*

through the window. Trae Vassallo lays bare the obstacles to overcome in venture and technology and shares how she bounced back from a negative experience. Stephanie Palmeri's story is one of total bravery and creativity when it came to getting a seat at Uncork Capital.

CHAPTER 2

THE ELEPHANT IN
THE VALLEY

——

So… How bad is it?

"Experiences included being groped by my boss while in public at a company event. After learning this had happened to other women in my department, and then reporting the event to HR, I was retaliated against and had to leave the company."

"I had a fellow VC sending me flowers, gifts, even a mixed tape, over the course of several months. Another portfolio CEO asked me to go through a door first so he could 'watch me walk,' and my superiors at the firm told me to laugh it off. I also had another VC tell me likes married women and put his hand on mine. (I'm married)"

"Example: I was propositioned by a hiring manager early in my career when I was a job candidate. He clearly indicated that if I slept with him, he would make sure I was promoted as his 'second in command' as he moved up the ladder in the company. I was lucky to have the option to reject the offer."

Silicon Valley is supposed to be a bastion of modern values, progressive people, and liberal attitudes. Yet why is it so hard for women to feel respected in the workplace? There is some scary shit from the report that shared these experiences: Elephant in the Valley. It is not like these women were bottom-of-the-food-chain either. "We asked 200+ women focusing on women with at least ten years of experience. The survey is largely Bay Area with 91 percent in the Bay Area/Silicon Valley right now. We have broad age ranges with 77 percent forty-plus and 75 percent have children. Our respondents hold positions of power and influence with 25 percent being CXOs, 11 percent being Founders, 11 percent being in venture. In addition to capturing start-up data, we also have employees from large companies including Apple, Google, and VMWare."[12]

---

12 Vassallo, Trae, Ellen Levy, Michelle Mandansky, Hillary Mickell, Bennett Porter, Monica Leas, and Julie Oberweis. 2018. "The Elephant In The Valley". *Elephantinthevalley.Com.*

Some statistics and anecdotes shared from Elephant in the Valley:

84 percent have been told they are too aggressive (with half hearing that on multiple occasions)

47 percent have been asked to do lower-level tasks that male colleagues are not asked to do

90 percent witnessed sexist behavior at company off-sites and/or industry conferences

88 percent have experienced clients/colleagues address questions to male peers that should have been addressed to them.

- On one of those stories: "In evaluating deals, sometimes a male CEO will address all his replies to my male associate while I'm the GP on point. I don't make investments in those companies."

Forty percent feel the need to speak less about their family to be taken more seriously.

Of those who took maternity leave, 52 percent shortened their leave because they thought it would negatively impact their career:

- "In one review session, one male partner said of a female employee 'we don't have to worry about her bonus or promotion because she just got married. So she'll probably have a baby and quit soon'"
- "While I was on maternity leave, a colleague tried to poach my team. I returned to a team that was distressed because they felt unprotected during my maternity leave during a particularly political time at our company (just post-IPO). In talking to other female execs, I think there is generally a concern that absence opens up teams and roles for poaching, which is unacceptable practice."
- "I had two kids twenty months apart. When I told my boss about the second pregnancy, his response was, 'Oh my god! Didn't you just have a baby?' By the way, he had three kids. When I returned from my second maternity leave, the mood was different, and there was little effort to include me in the flow of things. I was no longer part of the discussion on the cool big game-changer project, and my boss was complaining about how little my team had accomplished that summer. I had to remind him repeatedly that I hadn't been around, and there was no backfill, so how could anything have been done?"

60 percent of women in tech reported unwanted sexual advances

65 percent of women who report unwanted sexual advances had received advances from a superior, with half receiving advances more than once

60 percent who reported sexual harassment were dissatisfied with the course of action

39 percent of those harassed did nothing because they thought it would negatively impact their career

30 percent did not report because they wanted to forget

29 percent signed a non-disparagement agreement

* * *

Though the dominating culture is very male-centered, finance and venture capital is a relationship-driven business. Thus even if you feel alienated as the minority female it is important to acclimate to some part of that culture in order to have support from colleagues. Even if the men you work with might say something that rubs you the wrong way, it is important to speak up for yourself but not to antagonize the other person. You might have to play along for some time, and while that's frustrating at the time, doing that allows you to move up the ladder and open the doors for more women. Several VCs I spoke with have reiterated this point.

Joelle Kayden is the founder and Managing Member of Accolade Partners. Accolade Partners isn't a traditional VC fund because it invests in other funds rather than start-ups. As a fund of funds, Accolade has weathered the dot-com bubble and the 2008 crisis. Prior to founding Accolade in 2000, Joelle was the first CFO of ABS Ventures and then joined the Investment Banking Division of Alex. Brown & Sons where she was a managing director. She's a Stanford Graduate School of Business alumna and serves on the GSB's Advisory Council—involved with a number of initiatives to encourage women to pursue careers in investment management.[13]

Joelle is a seasoned veteran of the male-dominated world of finance and venture. When Joelle began her career journey, workplace culture was much less progressive than it is today. The world definitely hasn't solved gender inequality, but Joelle joked that back then, "There were no women and I had children." Joelle took five weeks of maternity leave.

"My company was growing really fast at the time and I was a good contributor. There were CEOs of companies who didn't want to work with women. And there are mentors who are men who have made my career a success. You just shrugged your shoulders and moved on. It is much more polarized today. People said things and if they were out of

---

13 "TEAM". 2018. *Accolade Partners.*

line you would say something. Maybe I'm eternally optimistic, but some of my biggest helpers were men. Those people saw somebody who worked hard and was smart and wanted to help them. A couple of people internally sponsored me and clients externally. In investment banking, you're always trying to get deals. Sponsorship and making sure someone went to bat for you. That's what men do. You find clients. You need both people internally and externally."

Another way to illustrate this concept is from my conversation with Julia Klein, an associate from Greenspring Associates who was headed to Harvard Business School when I last spoke to her. She told me that venture capital is a relationship-driven business. Sometimes that might mean that you have to show that you can hang. "Deals don't happen at the desk. They happen at dinners. Maybe your colleagues think that means knocking back some beers while at a game. Well… sure I can do that. It might not be exactly how I want to be spending my Saturday, but it is important to build the trust and relationships there."

While Ann Miura-Ko, founding partner of Floodgate, has paved the road for a lot of women, she is also very frank about progress in gender equality in the work culture of venture capital. Men usually are not out to get you, and when women correct men on inappropriate behavior, they're not out to get men either.

"I have the fortune of having the coworkers I do. If they say something sexist, they know I don't believe they are a bad person. It is only a problem when you think the person across the table from you is actually a bad person. It gets tense because hard to vet if everyone in your company is a good person or not. I think there's a high bar, but it is a bar you want to demand. There are female networks now where their reputation in venture capital is critical for a guy's success as well. If [men in venture capital] are painted in a sexist light by women, it becomes a real issue for them. Part of it is no giving feedback from a place of hurt. Try to figure out the awareness of that person. Try to figure out why they are the way they are. More than half the situations I've seen or heard about are where the person was oblivious. A part of it is helping educate key members—making sure that they know so they don't repeat those mistakes."

Is there a better alternative than the "just deal with it" approach? Yes, but it also requires that you have reached a position where you have the privilege of options to choose from.

One of the authors of Elephant in the Valley was Trae Vassallo, a former general partner at Kleiner Perkins. This is her story.

TRAE VASSALLO: A GOOD CULTURE PAYS ITSELF OFF. IF YOU'RE STUCK JUST ASK FOR HELP. PEOPLE ARE MORE THAN WILLING TO GIVE IT._

It began through the Kleiner Perkins v. Ellen Pao trial. Trae Vassallo, a Kleiner Perkins general partner of eleven years was subpoenaed to testify. During her testimony she had to talk about some of her experiences in the workplace, one of which was harassment.

"I had a number of folks that said wow thanks for sharing, I had a similar experience. I was shocked by the number of people who told me that and I'm shocked people don't talk about it often."

At first, Trae just felt so alone. However, she soon found that everyone felt that way, like they did something wrong for sharing their story. While it was a comfort that she wasn't alone, that illuminated how this is a massive problem. It is a massive problem and no one's talking about it. After Ellen Pao v. Kleiner Perkins Caufield and Byers, Trae and a cohort of successful women put out a survey to two hundred very experienced women.

"Over 60 percent have been sexually harassed in their career. Yeah okay, this is a problem. It was just one of the first times we had some of these numbers. The idea is not to point fingers or make a salacious headline but at least say, 'hey this is a problem.' Women are finally coming forward, and boards are taking action on bad behavior, helping move conversation forward where people aren't afraid and use the media to this advantage."

Trae ended up leaving KPCB right before the trial and didn't know what she was going to do next. She wanted to continue to do what she loved so she started seed investing to stay in the flow and connect with entrepreneurs. It forced her to reassess: "What do I care about? What makes me happy? What gives me meaning? What do people value in me? Was it just the Kleiner name and the checkbook?"

It turns out that Trae cared about investing based on the right culture. Trae's seed investing taught her that people do care about what she has to say. She grew the confidence to start a new fund and a new culture with the right partners. Partners like Neil Sequiera, who was like Trae and had spent a great number of years in the industry yet wanted to do something slightly different. Slightly earlier stage investment and, as it turns out, exceptional company cultures became their sweet spot.

"What set us apart were references and what people say about us. All my referencing on Neil showed that he just clearly treats people with a lot of respect. I wanted a partner who is a great human being in the good times and the bad. It came through while we were fundraising even though we're returns focused. It just keeps coming back that we're good people. We really connect with people and treat them respectfully. Work hard. A scrappy work ethic—that's important. A lot of folks in this industry don't work really hard for the early series A when the companies need a lot of help. We want to be able to."

As Reid Hoffman explained in his podcast "Masters of Scale," every employee in a company has to opt into their culture from the very beginning. A company that starts out with bad principles doesn't suddenly clean up once they get bigger. They just become larger versions of their preexisting selves. At Defy, Trae and Neil created this fund so there is no sexual harassment, so that there is diversity, and so that their values trickle down into the kinds of investments they make. Despite their combined twenty-four years of GP expertise at the crème de la crème of VC firms, Trae and Neil have no speck of elitism. They're so down to earth and focused on doing right by their investments and their LPs that they don't wait for companies to come to them. They go to the companies.

"One thing we like to do is meet companies at their offices. People are more relaxed and you get to see people interacting with each other. We've turned down investment opportunities once we saw the culture in the office. If it is shaky, we don't have time to be replacing CEOs and organizations. We want to back people in great leadership with strong cultures. A strong culture is a strategic advantage. It will weather far better than a mercenary culture."

That's just how culture-driven this fund is. Trae will invest when the company just loves what they're building and they love the mission so much they'll bust down walls to make it right for the customer. That's the kind of culture Defy wants. It is not busting down walls at all costs.

If there's any other lesson Trae has learned throughout her career in male-dominated industries, it is to ask for help because people love to give it. Way before she was a GP at Kleiner, Trae was in Stanford getting a masters in engineering. She had worked at IDEO where she got to engineer some amazing things like the Palm 5.

"It inspired me that the CEO of Palm Computing was Donna Dabinsky. It was the first time seeing a woman CEO and at a start-up company. I thought, 'Wow I want to do what she's doing. How do I do that?' I figured business school was probably a good move. I went to Stanford with the sole intention of becoming a start-up person."

One day John Doerr came to class and Trae had to collect the nerve to go talk to him. Part of business school was building the confidence to say, "Hi." The cool thing is that she had an ask. It was 1999 at the time and the internet was going crazy. Trae asked, "I know everyone is excited about the internet and I built the Palm 5 and I'm excited to bring hardware to the next level. What are you seeing that I could help start and get involved in?"

The hot shot Partner at Kleiner Perkins didn't hesitate to connect Trae to a couple of folks, and together they started Good Technology. When you ask people for something you need help with, realize that people (men and women) love to help if they can. If you're specific enough to ask for help and put yourself out there, that increases your chances of success too.

Trae cofounded the company and grew it to three hundred people. She was in charge of the hardware side of the business, which crashed pretty hard in 2002. Good Technology decided to run software on trios, which was a hardware platform. So Trae's part of the business was going away. Then, John asked what Trae was doing next.

"John asked what I was going to do and I said, 'I don't know but if I'm with you I should be good.'" I became an Entrepreneur in Residence at KPCB and then turned into an associate and then a partner role. I got the chance to work with forty different companies and work on incredible investments like Nest and Dropcam before I left in 2014."

It is not just about women entrepreneurs. It is about women engineers, board members, investors, etc. We need more women everywhere in tech. When we have more women everywhere in tech, we'll have more CEOs. Trae explains, "I like places where it is easy to put people in who happen to be female. One of the first companies we invested in, the first independent board member was an incredibly talented woman, and I can find these companies partly because my network is partly women. Look at your calendar. Who are you meeting with? Is it a diverse set of people? If you keep meeting with guys, you're not meeting with a diverse set of people."

ACTION ITEMS AND EXERCISES

DIVERSITY RE-EVALUATION

- Try diversifying the people you normally meet. Are you meeting with people from the same gender, race and interests? If you're a computer science student who only meets other computer science students, try hanging out with someone who is a government major. If you're Asian and you only hang out with other Asians, try meeting people outside your ethnicity. Don't be a double standard!

DISCUSS!

- Elephant in the Valley is as powerful as it is because a band of women decided to discuss the harassment and bring light to that problem. Have a discussion with people that have similar interests to you. What's the consensus about gender dynamics in business in your friend group? Brainstorm ways to have your voices heard and contribute to the dialogue together.

CHAPTER 3

GETTING OFF THE FLOOR... LITERALLY.

———

Venture capital is by nature a very risky business. You're betting that the sliver of your investment will be the one that returns the funds an assortment of rich and powerful people trusted you with and more. Yet only one out of ten start-ups will succeed, which means that the successful one needs to have a ten times return on investment in order to cover the loss of capital of the nine losers—just to break even. And you have to give the return back within ten years typically. It is not for the weak-stomached.

Stephanie Palmeri, I found, is anything but the sort. In fact, right after completing business school at Columbia University, she took a risk many would be appalled to attempt. She packed her two suitcases and without a job offer in VC, flew out of New York and settled down on her friends' floor in the Silicon Valley for two weeks. She didn't know anyone, save a few business school friends, and hadn't worked in venture for the first decade of her career.

What was she doing making this risky cross-country move? There was no guarantee she'd find a job in the exclusive and foreign environment of venture capital in the Silicon Valley. The time spent searching, money spent moving, and emotional commitment may have all been for naught. Most business school graduates are a shoo-in for higher-level banking and consulting positions. Why give that up for something much less common—venture capital?

"When I moved out I told myself—I came out in July 2011— I'd give myself till October to get out there and maybe find some side projects to work on and try to figure out who's hiring and how I can get in front of the right people who are making those hiring decisions. And it was tough because I knew a lot of folks were on vacation. It wasn't going to pick up until the end of August. My goal was to get the lay of the land, get out there and meet people by October to check in with myself and at that point ask myself if I have something or do I need to shift gears? I had done a lot of deliberate things to get closer to where I wanted to be such that when the time was right things fell in place."

It wasn't obvious that was going to work out. Stephanie wasn't sure if she would come out of business school and be an operator at a start-up again or if she would go the venture route. However, knowing the odds and still being willing to play, Stephanie showed an ability to assess risks and manage expectations. Certainly, Stephanie had real work experience under her belt and had worked across a number of different industries. She had been everything from an analyst at Accenture and a promotional programming manager at Clinique to a senior consultant at MKTG Inc. by the time she had entered business school. While there, she did an internship for venture capital while at business school that made her realize she thrived in venture capital. She genuinely enjoyed working with entrepreneurs and thought she had an aptitude for it. But it is a tricky business to break into. She had lived in New York at the time. Actually her entire life was spent on the East Coast. It was a tough decision to leave New York and move to California.

In 2011 there were not that many funds in New York and there were very few folks hiring at the post-MBA level. When Stephanie was at Columbia, there were maybe zero to three post-MBA roles in any given year in New York.

"I recognized I would have to expand my search. But I also recognized that in venture capital, a vast majority of dollars and a vast majority of the deals are in the Silicon Valley. I believe it was a gap in my experience and network to not have relationships out here. Whether or not that might bring me back to New York at some point in time, being in the valley for a certain amount of time was important. I moved out here with two suitcases and no job, and thanks to the kindness of a couple of my business school classmates, who let me sleep on floors and couches and what not, I was able to start networking here."

That networking paid off. After staying on her friend's floor for two weeks, she met the founder of what was then SoftTech VC—which was undergoing a change from a $15M fund to a $50M fund. Initially, Jeff Clavier responded to Stephanie by giving her career advice suggesting that she pursue venture capital at a later stage in her career. After asking to meet in person and telling him that she'd moved to California, he finally agreed to meet.

"I sat down with him, and he said to me, 'So, I'm supposed to convince you to not work in venture.' And I looked at him and said, 'Well yeah, but I just got here, and I'm pretty stubborn, so I'm going to try for a couple of months at least. But why don't we talk about start-ups?'"

Jeff Clavier respected Stephanie's bold move from New York to California. He offered her not a job but an opportunity. Stephanie would have eight weeks with SoftTech, and if she could prove she was needed, she'd have a job. He asked if she could start that day, and after four weeks she received a full-time offer.

"The thing that resonated with Jeff was the sheer confidence and determination it took to say, 'Hey I believe in myself and I will figure out a path regardless of how hard it is.' I do early stage investments, and I'm working with founders who are just getting their companies off the ground. And when I think about the types of founders I work with, there's a lot of similarities to that. My founders have had to believe in themselves when no one else sees the world the way they see it. I think that was what probably struck [Jeff]. He saw a determination and a will to do this work. The action of getting on a plane and moving across the country was probably a pretty big signal there."

Does everyone who wants to work in venture have to make a big dramatic move? No, but the lesson here is that you have to show that you care to be heard. And it doesn't hurt to be present when the right opportunity comes along.

"I think one of the challenges in venture is that the jobs aren't necessarily visible. First, firms aren't necessarily hiring when they bring people on board in venture. In many ways firms hiring in venture is very opportunistic. You realize there might be a need to bring someone on board or need someone who you think could be a great fit to the organization, and it is the right time to consider bringing someone in. That's what happened to me at SoftTech, which we now call Uncork Capital. I met our founder Jeff as the fund was in the process of going from a fifteen-million-dollar fund to a fifty-five-million-dollar fund. He had brought on another partner six to twelve months before I came on board in 2010 and yet there was still opportunity as the fund was growing. They had two partners and there was still just a ton of deals flow coming in. A lot of things needed to be done within the firm and portfolio that there was now potential need for someone else on the investment team. So my timing was really good."

Don't be fooled. Stephanie didn't simply take a huge risk and succeed because she struck it lucky. Though luck is a part of every success, Stephanie is masterful in crafting a strong network and that's what helped her land a job at Uncork Capital with the founder Jeff Clavier.

The second thing that worked in Stephanie's favor was that she had been building her network over the course of her years in New York and she had quite an overlap with Jeff's network. She got an introduction to Jeff through one of the firm's limited partners who was in her Columbia Business school network.

"More importantly, I think when Jeff went back to reference me he reached out to mutual connections, and they were people who knew me quite well. And so even if Jeff and I didn't know each other, there was a level of trust in the validation that came from those references. And those weren't references I provided him on a sheet of paper. Those were people he looked out to on his own. I wouldn't say that was intentional but I'm smart about how I build my network. The work you do will eventually speak for itself. That's true as you progress in your career as a venture capitalist. When you're a junior person in a firm and you're going head to head trying to win a deal against a partner at another firm, how do you do that? You need entrepreneurs who stand up and say, 'I want to work with that person.' It is fantastic that it happened but I think it needs to happen continuously as you grow in venture. You need to be creating value for people and demonstrating the strength of your work and your ideas. Be able to not just share them directly but also know there are people who will help reinforce that message."

Stephanie clearly had an advantage through her strong, supportive network. What did she do prior to moving that created such a network? How do other people build such an ecosystem of sharing references through their careers?

"If you look at the background of partners, you begin to realize they come from lots of different places. Maybe the more typical paths are a successful founder or the path having been in venture their whole career and they've grown that way, but plenty of people are nontraditional. They're PhD students, reporters, operators who were never founders, etc. You'll meet ex-military people, and a lot of different folks. I think what makes for strong partners is actually people with diverse backgrounds because you're pulling on that from a decision-making standpoint. Which is obviously one of the challenges when you look at firms that have really similar profiles amongst all their partners. Same exact resumes, same exact school you're going to get a lot of groupthink potentially."

One obvious thing to point out is that not everyone can or has the guts to make a transnational move to pursue their dreams. I think this is an important point here. While saying Stephanie did this out of nowhere to pursue her goals would be romantic, it is also not true. She had been working for several years in various industries and had a business school degree under her belt. Stephanie started her career as a consultant in technology and management consulting and did marketing for a number of years as an operator before doing some work in a start-up company in New York. She then leveraged her time in business school to make a career change into venture. I was curious how else Stephanie prepared herself for her uncertain path.

"I had six to eight years of working experience before going back to business school. I knew I wanted to take a shift career-wise and I didn't want to do the shift most MBA students would make to higher positions in banking or consulting. I knew stepping into school with that goal meant that my career search would have to be self-driven. I set for myself a number of checkpoints. If my end goal was to win a job in venture capital in the future and maybe even after that, I asked myself: what steps do I think I'll need to get there and what are the shorter term goals that'll allow me to get the skills I need to succeed? Like hey, get an internship in venture and see if it is something you like and want to do. And then thinking about whether your story would resonate with people who want to give you that job."

So we've heard all about how to strategically increase your chances of getting a job in venture by building your network, but what makes you a good VC? What is Stephanie's secret sauce, so good that Jeff Clavier didn't even wait for the end of the eight-week period before making her part of his firm?

"When I think about what makes someone a good fit for a firm, at a non-partner position, I think it is bringing a perspective on the types of investments the firm does. It is how they will be helpful not only in sourcing and evaluating deals but also supporting and helping companies. A good VC can help on all of those fronts, but maybe not from day one.

Maybe you walk in the door with the network and develop the ability to support portfolio companies. Maybe you walk in the door with "I'm a fantastic operator" and you're going to be really supportive and build a network leveraging the brand of the fund. But those are the three core things a good investment professional needs to do and needs to develop over time. The top of the funnel is the sourcing of deals, the kind of evaluation of whether we want that deal in the funnel or not, and then getting to close the deal and see it through to the end."

When you think about entry-level jobs in venture, the analyst roles, there's really not a lot to distinguish any one candidate from anyone else. The reality is that most analysts are learning on the ground. Firms are looking for a certain level of aptitude in terms of evaluating business models and a certain amount of EQ in terms of being able to spend time with founders. As one goes up the ladder at their first job, funds are looking for skills to be more developed. They're potentially looking for more of a track record. If a fund is looking to fill an entry-level position, the questions are probably not "What deals did you source at your last fund?" or "What deals did you lead?" However, as you move up the ladder, that becomes increasingly important.

The greatest lesson from Stephanie's story is that in order to get into an industry that doesn't have a conventional recruiting pipeline, you'll need to learn to make bold moves and be confident in yourself. Stephanie's bravery goes beyond moving from one coast to another. Reaching out to Jeff Clavier even after he had given her a big fat no takes a lot of bravery to put herself out there for judgment again. Her insistence was also only possible because she *knew she was qualified enough to push it. Jeff reaching out to her colleagues and references and being convinced himself proves that point.*

ACTION ITEMS AND EXERCISES

PEOPLE REMEMBER YOU FOR RISKS YOU TAKE

Taking a risk, like moving across the country without a confirmed job offer, shows passion and willingness. Pick something risky, but reasonable and challenge yourself to start working on it by the end of the week. Here's a framework to think about:

- Take some time to write down all the things you've wanted to do, but haven't done yet.
- For each item, list the risks associated with it and why you attempted it.
- Take a look at the reasons and risks you've written down and re-evaluate each one. If you take the risk, ask yourself what is the worst that could happen?

BE CONFIDENT IN YOUR VALUE-ADD

You can only confidently market yourself if you know your skills. Try this exercise:

- List all your hard skills but then ask yourself why you are uniquely qualified to evaluate something. Why does your opinion hold weight? This could be because of a past internship that had something to do with evaluating start-ups. This could be because you learned about a specific model in class in depth, etc. Think about why you have the chops for the job. If there's something you genuinely feel you need that is glaringly obvious in order to make better decisions, start taking an online course for it by the end of week! You don't need to learn everything there is to know about financial modeling to feel confident. One new skill a week or month will lead you to feel more comfortable marketing yourself.

- If you've applied for something or wanted to speak with someone and get an initial "no," don't see that as the end game! Try speaking with that person again from a different angle. Insistence can lead to your dream opportunity.

PART II

WHAT WE'RE DOING

CHAPTER 4

IT'S IN THE DETAILS.

———

The pipeline problem argues that there are not enough qualified women in the hiring pipeline to pick from. Have you met Ann Miura-Ko? I beg to differ. I have never met anyone else whose academic and professional life embodies absolute excellence as much as hers.

No matter how large or small the task or expectation, no one does perfection better than Ann Miura-Ko.

ANN MIURA-KO: BE WILLING TO UNCLOG THE TOILET AT YOUR FUND

Ann Miura-Ko is a self-proclaimed "ninja-assassin investor" and dubbed "the most powerful woman in start-ups" by *Forbes. Oh, and also the partner and co-founder at*

Floodgate Capital with Mike Maples, an investor famous for his bets on Twitter, Chegg and other digital successes. From electrical engineering at Yale to working at McKinsey and a PhD in math at Stanford, Miura-Ko had a unique mix of experiences before she started Floodgate—a seed and early stage fund. Since then Miura-Ko has made successful bets on Mod-Cloth, Lyft, Ayasdi, Xamarin, Refinery29, TaskRabbit, and JoyRun. She first debuted on the Midas List last year before returning to the list again in 2018.[14] *The Midas List, Forbes' list of the top one hundred most influential investors, only boasts five women investors. And in March of 2017, Floodgate had just closed its sixth fund at $131 million dollars.*[15]

So how did she get from electrical engineering to venture capital? She changed careers more times than she could count while in college.

"It is important to get a lot of context to figure out what you're really good at and what you're not good at. I know that can be hard because good is so relative. To me it was like something was out there in the world that I could be exceptional at, better than 99 percent of the people out there. Once you think about that, you find the right set of

---

14 Chaykowski, Kathleen. 2018. "Meet The Top Women Investors On Midas In 2018". *Forbes*.

15 Loizos, Connie. 2018. "Floodgate Closes Sixth Fund With $131 Million". *Techcrunch*.

investors or mentors who can really see the future version of you. And invest in that. I also invested in what I felt were my strongest skillsets.

"Here's an example of where I wasn't a fit. I grew up thinking I was going to be a medical doctor, but when I compared myself to my best friend, an incredible hematology and oncology doctor, I can see she has a deeper sense of empathy. She loves helping people and has a passion for the science of medicine that I didn't. When I was in academia at Stanford for my PhD, certain professors were super young and were my age, and I could see they were the top of their class in terms of everything they needed to do to be super successful. While I was good, I wasn't at that level. The great thing about being able to calibrate by surrounding yourself with and seeing people truly excellent at what they do is that you know what you're capable of."

While going through this calibration, two key mentors also helped ferry her down the path she would eventually take. Lew Platt and Mike Maples, two Silicon Valley big shots, have shaped the career path of Miura-Ko.

In college, Miura-Ko worked in the dean's office of engineering. She ended up showing a surprise visitor around campus—Lewis Platt, the CEO of Hewlett Packard from 1992 through 1999.

"He invited me to follow him and shadow him during my spring break," says Miura-Ko. So, as a Palo Alto native, she took him up on that proposal and went to the HP office in the Bay Area. After that, Platt did something that would forever change the way Miura-Ko thought about her potential.

"When I returned to my college campus, he had sent me two pictures," says Miura-Ko. "One was a picture of myself, sitting next to Lew and talking to him. The second picture was Bill Gates, who had visited that week. He was sitting exactly where I had sat. People have literally put a picture in my head of who I should be and have caused me to believe in things that I probably wouldn't have about myself."

Miura-Ko's opportunity with Lew Platt may seem lucky, but it is not coincidental. The takeaway here is that Miura-Ko grew her opportunities with an incredibly purposeful work ethic. She conveys her motivation and vision—never holding back her desire to participate in even the littlest tasks in her journey toward success. The desire is often most convincing to a person's clients, partners, and potential employers. Her NASA rocket scientist dad taught her to be world-class at everything. And when I say everything, I mean everything.

"No job is too small. When I first started Floodgate, if I had to unclog the toilet I had to unclog the toilet. You don't think 'Well I'm a partner here at Floodgate so I don't have to do that.'" Miura-Ko explains. Dissociating yourself from your title means you never miss any opportunities because you'll never say no to something.

"There's a sense of wonder that is certainly freeing and you want to feel that way about everything. As a young person you can get caught up in an 'I want' perspective. For example: I want a big respected job. But if people can't trust you with a small job, why would they try to trust you with a big one? Really treat every small thing like it is incredibly important to you."

Having just joined a firm and proving herself with her first deal, Ann felt grateful that entrepreneurs also took a bet on her the way she took a bet on them.

"For me that was when I invested in Leah Busque. She was sort of one of these first investments. I saw in Leah the brand idea that really excited me as a person capable of building a product, what it would look like, and why it existed. I felt like I had to work with her. I didn't want Mike to invest because I wanted to invest in her. It was a real connection. At the time I was four months pregnant and in many senses it was a time when everything was happening at once. If you combine everything you had to accomplish in one, it might sound like a lot, but if you take it one day at a time one hour at a time—it is surprising how much one person can do. It was really a confidence-building moment because so much happened in a year."

Trying to begin a career in an industry where there are few role models to look up to, or applying to companies where women are not really represented can be really difficult. However, that also means that the 8 percent of women who held those positions in 2017 got there somehow. While 8 percent is bad, 8 percent also means male mentors and colleagues exist to help shape the careers of these successful women and get them to where they are today.

"I remember asking one of the partners if there were any women they knew in this industry, and they didn't," Miura-Ko tells CNBC's Julia Boorstin. "There isn't a multitude of people where you could just point to that person and say, 'That's the person I am going to be in ten, twenty, thirty years.' And I think that's tough."

Being unable to put a picture in your head where a woman like you can make it in a venture capital firm can be a real barrier to succeeding in venture capital. However, a lack of women represented in venture didn't faze Miura-Ko. She's been involved in male-dominant fields every step of her career.

"I think an issue with these male-dominated firms is they are very open to having women, but women don't perceive that to be the truth, so they may not apply," Miura-Ko said. "Or even if they apply and get the position, they question how they'll fit in. That ends up being more of the issue from what I've heard from other potential female partners interviewing at firms that only have men. 'Do I really want to be the first female there, and is that really setting myself up for success?' I'm used to being one of two women in the room. From the time I was in college I was majoring in electrical engineering where it was already a small major, less than thirty people, but there were only two women. Getting into McKinsey, it was forty analysts my year and probably five or six were women. It is not that unusual for me to be in a situation where there aren't that many women. The dynamic there didn't faze me. I was lucky when it came to Floodgate. It wasn't that I was joining an existing organization. I was creating with a co-founder. The first two years were just the two of us so we were naturally gender-neutral."

Now, Miura-Ko has become the partner women picture when they think of making it into the small number of female partners in venture capital.

"Our initial hires were all women—an admin and a female CFO. A couple of associates were some of the first male folks we brought in to the fold. One of our first partner hires was a woman. For a while, our senior people were mostly women. We weren't looking for more women but more women applied. Probably 80 percent of our resumes were from women. It was interesting to me because women tend to feel like they can apply for a position where there are already are women. They feel more welcome there."

After six years as a female founding partner of a successful firm, Miura-Ko has a comprehensive and thoughtful perspective on the matter of gender-equality and gender relations in venture capital.

"Part of [the lack of women partners] is that it is an access problem. I think this is gradually changing, but you had to go up and down Sandhill road. You had to have a warm intro and be one step removed but there was no digital or social network. So that's changing because a) there are way more firms b) there's much more information out there, and c) there are incubators. There are lots of different ways you can access capital. That's a low-level change. We do see that where there are female investors we get more female founders than at a male-only firm. There's a comfort to approaching investors who are women."

While Miura-Ko's career has paved the road for a lot of women, she is also very frank about progress in gender equality in the work culture of venture capital. Men usually are not out to get you, and when women correct men on inappropriate behavior, they're not out to get men either.

"I have the fortune of having the coworkers I do. If they say something sexist, they know I don't believe they are a bad person. It is only a problem when you think the person across the table from you is actually a bad person. It gets tense because hard to vet if everyone in your company is a good person or not. I think there's a high bar, but it is a bar you want to demand. There are female networks now where their reputation in venture capital is critical for a guy's success as well. If [men in venture capital] are painted in a sexist light by women, it becomes a real issue for them. Part of it is no giving feedback from a place of hurt. Try to figure out the awareness of that person. Try to figure out why they are the way they are. More than half the situations I've seen or heard about are where the person was oblivious. A part of it is helping educate key members—making sure that they know so they don't repeat those mistakes."

The lack of women in venture and entrepreneurship will not be solved simply by employing more female partners— though that is a necessary step.

"What we do need more of is women starting companies that are not necessarily gendered and not approaching a gendered product for females. We need more generalized consumer applications enterprise software founded by women. We need women who are involved in watching start-ups."

Her argument makes sense. Humans are naturally inclined to surround themselves with the kind of people that most resemble themselves. If you are a male interested in venture capital and all you see are other males around you, you're more likely to subconsciously exclude women from your circles without meaning to. If you are a female and never in the same activities in high school nor the same majors in college, males in those spaces won't know you're interested in the same things or qualified to work in them.

Miura-Ko advises female students at Stanford who want to work with start-ups to get into mixed gender study groups. A lot of start-ups begin all male because those are the guys sitting around the dorm room when they start. "It doesn't just occur to them to have a woman," she says. "They have to know you exist."

Which is why women being part of STEM companies and traditionally more "male" sectors are important. I once spoke with Amy Millman, who is the CEO of Springboard Enterprises, an investment catalyst organization that helps investors find women-led businesses. Her company has been around since 2000 and has dealt with $8B worth of funds over the lifetime of the company. Millman explained how in the dot-com era few women were represented in entrepreneurship because women mostly created products that were consumer-facing. At that time, investors were focused on hardware and business-to-business enterprises so they never invested in consumer-facing, e-commerce businesses that women led. It was not that there are more women entrepreneurs now than there were back then, but that investments now have shifted to prefer e-commerce and consumer-facing products, which more women represent.

"I think there is a problem where if you're not investing in a certain sector, you might not encounter any female founders. We need to encourage more women in a lot of other areas where we may not find as many female founders as male founders like in enterprise software."

Stand out by showing up where no one else does. Men have to know you exist. You have to elect to sit at the boys' table.

ACTION ITEMS AND EXERCISES

GET INTO THE HABIT OF BEING "WORLD CLASS"

Be extra. Take the little things seriously! In your internship or projects, volunteer to take on the tasks that have to be done but seem little, or tasks others may not want to do. Be meticulous about their execution. People always appreciate that. If you can't do the little things, why should people trust you with the big things?

SIT AT THE BOY'S TABLE

Venture capital is comprised of mostly men currently, whether we like that or not. Try to network with people of a different gender. If there's something you've always thought was cool and wanted to do, but didn't because it was mostly guys, try your hand at it! For example, coding camps or hackathons.

CHAPTER 5

GET NERDY, GO DEEP

————

Kirsten Green and Eurie Kim have been making a killing by focusing on an industry that has a heavily female audience: retail and commerce. An archaic industry ripe for change from the most innovative startups a.k.a a gold mine for venture investing.

If women are the future, why is it so hard to hire women to invest in them? Women in venture capital have had to be more qualified than their male peers to get the job. Like Stephanie Palmeri explained in the last chapter, often times women don't fit the conventional VC mold so they may have to outperform to prove themselves worthy of a role. In an interview with CNN Money Kirsten Green, founder of wildly successful Forerunner Ventures, put it this way, "There is a part of me that feels like I have to show up and be better and smarter and etc. all those things. Maybe that's not fair, but it is what it is a little bit, and that's not necessarily a bad thing."[16]

When I was in second grade, I remember my worldview was heavily impacted by two works in media: Mulan and The Cabin in the Woods.

First off, it was cool to me as an Asian American kid to see an Asian heroine in the Disney Princess series. I really believed when I was really young that I couldn't ever be the prettiest girl unless I was white (that's a whole other book). But more relevant to this topic is the fact that she defied all gender norms to contribute value to her country and family—an honor that was reserved for men at that time.

Laura Ingall's family also imparted the lesson that while the frontier is full of bears and wolves, being the first ones to settle means opening a way for others to experience something wonderful. (I'm thinking about that Christmas scene where the whole Ingalls family comes to their cabin and they have a jolly, classically American time).

When people think of VC they think that the portfolio companies are the entrepreneurial ones. We often forget

---

16 Draznin, Haley. 2018. "Venture Capitalist Kirsten Green: We Need More Women Founders". *CNNmoney.*

that starting a venture fund is just like starting a business and the founders like all other founders have to find a way to fundraise. It may be a cringe comparison but I've found my Mulan and Laura Ingalls in the world of venture capital investing: Forerunner Ventures.

FORERUNNER |ˈFÔRˌRƏNƏR|

noun: a person or thing that precedes the coming or development of someone or something else.

To me, Kirsten Green and Eurie Kim are truly forerunners—focusing their wildly successful fund strictly on companies redefining the consumer landscape—an endeavor that surprisingly no venture capital investor has ever done before. Their fund is like Laura Ingalls—opening up the frontier of venture investing in a completely overlooked market. And also like Mulan, discreetly entering the boys-only scene and then SURPRISE! The fund that cashed out when Jet.com sold to Walmart for a billion dollars is managed by mostly women. I liken their success to when Shang walked in on Mulan in that unwrapping scene and she was discovered to be -gasp- a woman but then she actually ends up winning the war for China.

Let me explain to you how incredibly this fund has performed. Since Forerunner's inception in 2010, the fund has raised a total of $658.6M across 5 funds, $360M of which is from their fourth and latest fund announced October 8th, 2018.[17] They've made 14 exits and have invested in some big-name winners:

The most notable amongst the firm's 14 exits to date:

1. Dollar Shave Club sold to Unilever for $1billion in 2016. Forerunner made an early stage investment into the company's $1million seed round, racking up an estimated 150x+ return.
2. Jet.com is bought by Walmart for $3 billion dollars in 2016.

Let me also specify that Forerunner is an early-stage fund, so they invested in Jet.com and Dollar Shave Club when they were pretty new. Therefore, the growth on their investments have been dramatic.

Kirsten and Eurie have also invested early in Warby Parker, Away Travel, and Glossier, a makeup company that has been named the most innovative beauty company and completely disrupted the beauty industry with their chic minimalist culture. Their marketing is so good, everyone's favorite celebrity and Instagram influencer is obsessed with it. If you're my age and you haven't heard of Glossier or the raving reviews celebrities have given it, you've been living under a rock.

---

17 "Forerunner Ventures Fund Overview". 2018. *Crunchbase.*

Why does a company like Glossier merit an investment from Forerunner? I wasn't exactly sure what was so disruptive and new about it until I visited their show room in SoHo.

First of all, who has a show room for makeup? Second of all, the entire experience was so incredibly consumer-centric. Sales reps wore unmistakeable pink jumpsuits, manned every podium of product, and would ring you up wherever in the store you were and bring your bag of curated goodies straight to you. There's no checkout line, no cash wrap. When I was purchasing my cream blush, a woman with chicly styled hair swiped my card asked me, "So how did you hear about Glossier?"

"Really who hasn't heard about Glossier? The marketing is so good whenever I see a sponsored post on Instagram it never feels like an ad."

"Wow thanks so much, I'm actually the head of marketing! Thanks for letting me know."

An executive of this brand is working the floor on Easter, checking out customers like everyone else, just to get a better understanding of the consumer and their experience. That's what it means to invest in a well-run company that is breaking retail's status quo.

Forerunner absolutely owns this market with their focus and long standing experience in the space. Prior to Forerunner, Kirsten was an equity research analyst and investor at Bank of America Securities, analyzing and investing in publicly-traded retail and consumer stocks.[18] She had a passion for fashion so strong it was nerdy. Eurie Kim is a Wharton Business School grad and former consultant at Bain & Company in their retail/consumer practice who had started her own luxury handbag company. No one knows the challenges and opportunities of a retail business more intimately than these two investors.

When asked what the critical factor to a successful startup is, Eurie says, "It takes a special founder. They don't have to be gregarious or good on TV, but rather, they need to be uniquely qualified to solve the problem they are looking to solve. Founders who are authentic in their mission, disciplined in being able to put a high caliber team together to execute on their vision, and capable of being able to draw people into their story, will often have a better outcome than those who may approach business building like a case study or analytical exercise."

Forerunner's way of looking at retail is well summed up in a talk Kirsten Green gave in 2017 with Recode. She took

18 "Green, Kirsten – Forerunner Ventures". 2018. *Forerunnerventures. Com.*

classic American brands like Sears, Macy's, Ralph Lauren, and Coca Cola and asked the audience whether they were retailers or brands. The audience had no problem determining: retailer, retailer, brand, brand. But then Green tried another set of more companies Apple, Warby Parker and Bonobos. The responses from the crowd this time were much less deliberate.

"The roles of brands and retailers used to be clear. They were complimentary but mostly distinct. In the past cycles, brands were identified most closely by product. They put beautiful images on them, they attached a logo to it and hopefully it was something iconic. Most of them didn't have a direct relationship with a consumer. Retailers, on the other hand, were all about context. They took those products, they put them in stores, they merchandised them, they invited customer into their environment and focused on servicing them and closing the transaction. Today's $22 Trillion retail ecosystem is being completely reorganized. It's being fueled by a customer's evolving taste in retail. It's not that we shop at any one location but rather many different channels. It's because we're constantly being inundated with triggers that affect our purchase decisions... the lines between retailers and brands are blurring. They're conflating and they're challenging economic models of the past."[19]

---

19 "Kirsten Green, Founder Of Forerunner Ventures, Explains How Retail Needs To Change | Code Commerce". 2018. *Youtube*.

As we all know, big box retailers have had a hard time recently growing as they used to. With the advent of online shopping, retailers like Sears are seeing store closures all over the country. **Between 2010 and 2013, visits to Malls decreased 50%.** Under Kirsten and Eurie's direction, Forerunner has rightly identified that the retail industry as being ripe for disruption, and their team is focused on investing in "next generation leaders who are reimagining the entire commerce ecosystem."

Forerunner and Rethink Impact's success drives home the point: *it pays to own the fact that you're a woman.* Own the fact that the majority of the market is represented by people like you. Own the fact that investing in women and in diversity is just lucrative.

ACTION ITEMS AND EXERCISES

FIND YOUR "NERDY" ELEMENT

Is there something that you like so much you truly wouldn't spend all day researching? Don't worry if it doesn't seem "business related." Whether it be the video gaming industry, the retail and fashion industry or sports, find something you don't mind becoming an expert in. Something you're nerdy enough about to want to know the business of companies that create the content you love.

CHAPTER 6

KNOW YOUR PRODUCT

———

Say you didn't graduate from business school and do a couple years on Wall Street. Are your chances of being a VC shot?

Absolutely not. If there's anything I learned it is that VCs come from all sorts of places. Though generally, if they're not the financial analysis type, they're qualified because of start-up operating experience or industry expertise. For example, Vanessa Larco is a Partner at NEA who has a background in product development in tech start-ups. Therefore, when she hears pitches on new tech companies, she can easily separate whether their product is defensible. Danielle Strachman (who we'll talk about next chapter) at 1517 fund is an expert in an unusual way—homeschool tutoring. That experience has given her an understanding of young entrepreneurs like no other VC. And lastly, I'll share the story of

Ann Weiss who hasn't let pregnancy stop her from being an entrepreneur twice, but has in fact allowed it to fuel her passion in the mom-market.

Taking a note from Stephanie Palmeri's story, VCs aren't really advertising that they're hiring, so you need to prove your value and prove that they need you. What can you bring to a team if you don't have financial experience? Try start-up experience or industry experience specific to the fund thesis.

VANESSA LARCO: KNOW THE TECH FROM THE INSIDE OUT

When I was searching for the female partners at top companies to interview, I kept running into this woman on LinkedIn. "Partner at New Enterprise Associates," her title said. I was confused why her bright smile and wrinkle-free face kept showing up in searches. She looked so young I thought she must have been my age, maybe a sophomore still in college. I later found that if she had been a college student, she'd be the most overqualified one I've ever met, having built products for Microsoft, Playdom, Box, Vanessa even started her own company FunLoop. And last but not least she has indeed become a partner at NEA.

Though any point on her resume is enough bragging rights for a lifetime, Vanessa replied to my email with incredulous humility. "I'm afraid I don't have great advice about transitioning from product management to venture capital as it was never part of my plan," she wrote back to me. "I just fell into it because I knew someone at this firm." I knew there would be a good story here—no average joe just gets picked up as a partner with zero investing experience. Especially not at a top Silicon Valley venture capital firm. Her path to partner is anything but conventional and she knows it too. "It looks like folks that planned on becoming VCs came from investment banking, private equity backgrounds," she commented.

Though she holds a strong background in engineering as a computer science major from Georgia Tech, Vanessa never became a software engineer. She wasn't thrilled about writing code all day every day but was excited about creating things.

Fortunately, Microsoft encouraged her to take on product management: "It was my junior year internship role," she reminisced. "In the middle of my software engineering interview, they asked me, 'Why are you interviewing for this and not product management?'" She had no idea what that was.

"In my CS classes I didn't know it but I naturally took on the PM role in my group. Everyone wanted to do the backend stuff. It was the sexy stuff. I actually liked the front end stuff and the PowerPoint presentation we would pitch that would actually give us the grade and the documentation to give to next semester's class to build off of. I didn't realize I was writing specs. When Microsoft told me what product management was, it was what I'd been already doing."

This was interesting. Here I was, trying to unlock the five-year plan to partner and everything Vanessa learned has shown that having systematic tunnel vision is the opposite of what you want. In fact, you may not even know that the perfect job for you exists, as was Vanessa's case. The importance of flexibility is a theme that would turn up again in Vanessa's career.

"I was so much more flexible in college and a few months into my job. Once I got to Microsoft I realized how much this is a system. There are levels and reviews and promotion cycles. I treated it maybe not like a game, but I was so prescriptive about it. I ended up working on some really good stuff but I also missed out on a lot. One of my friends was one of the first few engineers at Box, while it was still operating out of a garage. He asked me to join and immediately I told him absolutely not. It was not part of my five-year plan. I had this *plan*."

So much for that. After three years she moved on to two start-ups and cofounded her own. And then in 2014 things came full circle since her offer to join Box while at Microsoft.

"I ended up joining Box five years later," she chuckled. "I was so rigid and was planning every little aspect of my career that I stopped taking risks and doing things I thought were fun. In your twenties, you should absolutely be doing that."

Since Microsoft, it is clear that Larco has made some pretty great bets on the companies she's worked for. What leads her to where she is today is her desire to overcome greater and newer challenges despite their risks.

"Someone at NEA talked about what I wanted in my next role. After several months of brainstorming things, he made an offer to join. I thought it was crazy. It was a scary challenge and I didn't know what I was looking for."

Ironically that was exactly what she was looking for.

"I got to a point in my career where I wanted a new challenge, a big challenge. The best advice one of my mentors has given me is to take on a challenge that makes you slightly uncomfortable so you know you're stretching." Roles in product development, even at the most exciting companies, weren't an uncomfortable challenge for Larco. "Looking at other opportunities from where I was, it all seemed like more of the same stuff I had already done. I didn't see any scary challenge opportunities."

Reflecting on some of her colleagues like the friend at Box, Larco acknowledges how their risks have led them to great success:

"My roommate in college was a designer. She just said one day, 'I want to work on something! There are these two start-ups called Uber and Strava that I want to work at.' I was like oh whatever and she became the first designer at Uber. I thought she was crazy. I meet young people and everyone wants to have everything so planned out. I'm not sure if you can be the next Zuckerberg or Evan if you're going to become risk adverse."

The greatest lesson here, and I think this is especially applicable to us college kids gunning for a surefire consulting or banking gig post-grad, is that you hit it big when you take the risk. And really at post-grad, there's not much to lose.

"I read a book about what it takes to coach a successful child and it was interesting because they follow kids from affluent Northeast private schools and kids from the projects. The head of the schools from the Northeast was like, 'Look. We're not producing any Steve Jobs or presidents here. We're making consultants.' Everyone does well but no one is revolutionary. In the projects, they produce one Fortune 500 famous guy. These students have nothing to lose. As long as they have a house and food they've kind of made it. These folks in private schools have a lot to lose. They want at least upper-middle class, at least a home, and a nice car. Everyone goes to an Ivy League, graduates, and does two years with a socially acceptable career, gets an MBA and then…Crisis mode! They delay making big moves because it is scary and

I see that all the time. It doesn't surprise me. Ninety percent of Georgia Tech ends up going to consulting. It is a top engineering school and that's just where everyone goes except for CS majors. CS majors go to Microsoft, IBM, and a few people went to Facebook and Google and a bunch went to Apple. Nobody would do their own start-up that was just crazy talk."

A common argument is that working in a well-established firm in finance or consulting prepares you for jobs at start-ups. You build a network, a reputation associated with a name brand, and a specifically trained set of skills. Most of all, the opportunity cost of a name brand consulting or finance firm on a resume is too high to ignore. So the Georgetown story goes…

But Vanessa disagrees.

If Vanessa were still in college and if she had to do it all over again, she would do things differently. "Microsoft was valuable and I learned concrete skills. I could have done without it. If you asked me again after graduating if I would have joined Microsoft or Box I would have joined Box because you're on a rocket ship."

But Box is a really successful start-up. What if the start-up you work for doesn't become a rocket ship?

"You can go with your first six jobs at start-ups that don't work out. Most of the time you don't land on a rocket ship but you meet more people so fast and your odds increase so that eventually you will find the rocket ship."

Larco's story goes to show, that even in the elusive world of venture capital, you can go from zero to hero by being flexible enough to accept the right opportunities. Her experience in almost every aspect of entrepreneurship—from owning your her product to owning her own business—allows her to bring a different perspective to venture capital.

"I think we all have our backgrounds, not just professionally but culturally. All of that gives you different lenses to evaluate different opportunities. When I look at the company, I like to use and understand how the product integrates into someone's life. I start there and then think about the team. Would I be able to work with this team? If I wasn't in venture capital would I be able to join these people? I have an advantage in understanding product metrics and what they mean for the business and how much value that's giving."

Something that has been consistent between her mastery of product and her foray into venture is her experience on intensive collaboration. "You have to have a consensus about which products to build and what features to create. Similarly, you have to come to a conclusion with a team about what investments to make."

Before diving into this book I had trepidation around the idea that the skills needed to be a venture capital investor were only available to those with a background in finance. I was relieved to meet people with backgrounds like Vanessa and the women in the next few chapters.

ACTION ITEMS AND EXERCISES

CREATE SOMETHING!

Especially if you're not a huge finance person, try putting yourself in projects. Vanessa learned so much about teamwork, products, and operations by putting herself into those situations. Start small like a local hackathon and try to make something from scratch with a team. You don't need to be a coder to participate in a hackathon either. If you're not sure which one to go to, try the Major League Hacking site and look for one coming up near you: https://mlh.io/

TAKE PART IN THE START-UP COMMUNITY

If you don't want to code, hack, or do something tech, try being an operator at a friend's start-up or volunteering your time to help them. Be part of a team and learn how others make decisions.

CHAPTER 7

BE AN INDUSTRY SPECIALIST

Danielle Strachman: Entrepreneurs? Start 'Em Young!

I found 1517 Fund fascinating. In the VC world, investors liken winning investments to that of storybook creatures. Uber is a unicorn, Floodgate looks for thunderzillas, and people are now looking for dragons. All these analogies drive home how the potential of an investment must be so grand it is almost ~mythical~. I joked with Danielle Strachman from 1517 that we're running out of creatures and it's really refreshing to hear there's a micro-vc fund looking for their Martin Luther. The 1517 investment thesis reads:

"On October 31, 1517, Martin Luther nailed his Ninety-Five Theses to a church door in Wittenberg to protest the sale of indulgences. These were pieces of paper the establishment church sold at great cost, telling people it would save their souls. The church made a fortune doing it. Likewise, universities today are selling a piece of paper at great cost and telling people that buying it is the only way they can save their souls. Universities call it a diploma, and they're making a fortune doing it. Call us heretical if you like, but the 1517 Fund is dedicated to dispelling that paper illusion. Extraordinary careers are possible outside tracked institutions.[20]

"1517 marks a turning point in history where great social transformations were wrought by technology. Though Gutenberg's revolution had been in action for more than fifty years, the mass adoption and diffusion of the printing press meant Luther's message could influence all of Europe, and not only the people of a small town in Germany. Authority on questions of great importance no longer had to come from priests or royalty. It could come from books, and even more dangerously for the establishment, from an individual's own judgment. Many current technological and social trends point to our future rhyming with this past. We intend to make it so."

---

20 "Thesis". 2018. 1517 Fund. Accessed October 19 2018. http://www. 1517fund.com/thesis/.

Strachman gave me an example of a Martin Luther— a young man named Max Lock.

"We met him three or four years ago when he was eighteen and we were at the Thiel Fellowship before the fund started. We had this pitch competition where we would give them $100,000 to scale their business. He came up there and the first thing that came out of his mouth was, 'I want to disintermediate the freight shipping industry.' I remember just thinking whoa. He's eighteen and sure he looks pretty clean cut, but I did not expect those words to come out of his mouth. I thought, well what could you possibly know about that. Max said, 'I was fourteen and had an ice cream service. I was in a restaurant and they had just horrible, horrible ice cream.' He loved to cook, so he worked to make a much better ice cream recipe and started selling to people. Max ended up calling his company Schoolboy Ice Cream Company and started distributing at Whole Foods. It got to where he needed to get his cups and cones from China. He worked in a public high school that gave him a closet to work out of. Max even got kicked out of some business for students programs because he didn't believe in doing hypothetical business plans."

What Max noticed while doing his ice cream business is that working to get these cups cones was so challenging. He realized it could be much simpler. Really you could just have a tech layer, a website with a two-sided marketplace between a person who needs a product and a shipper. He pitched that to Strachman and her team and they gave him a $1,000 grant, which he would later turn into $100,000 when he became a Thiel Fellow. He built a landing page and took himself to Tech Crunch Disrupt SF and pitched to Marissa Mayer and Jeff Mayes. At eighteen. With no product and a landing page. He didn't win, but he got runner-up and someone who watched him pitch in the crowd was an investor interested in old businesses with new tech layers and told him he wanted to work with him. That became his first investor. He took an investment from that person and started building out the team.

"He thought about how he was going to build out a two-sided marketplace with people and freight shippers. So he got reviews for freight shippers and used that to build it out. Now he has a whole floor of a building in Oregon. It is pretty smart. You can buy a lot more office space there with the same money you could get a small shack in the Valley. One woman, when she was hired, said, 'Let's all go to happy hour!' And he had to say, "But I'm not twenty-one yet.' She couldn't believe it. 'I can't believe my boss is younger than me. My boss isn't old enough to drink.' They're called fleet. They've raised their series A and are working with twenty people—starting to expand and grow their business. Max has never stepped foot in a college. He's never thought about it because he doesn't need it to prove anything. He's a businessman through and through."21

Sure the world of venture capital is a risky one by nature, but specifically investing in dropouts? What would convince an investor that lack of experience offers a big enough upside that one could return their LP's money? Start-ups are evaluated on the quality of their team, whether or not their product achieves the right market fit, and other metrics that require real-world experience. Strachman, however, has the rare insight and career experience that has enabled her to find these hidden gems.

"I think I was listed or on record as one of the youngest school principals at twenty-six."

With an extensive background in alternative education systems, Strachman has had exposure to young adults unhindered by the boundaries of a conventional education system and the amazing projects they produce. She started out with a tutoring gig for homeschool students, which blossomed into a small business, which led to the creation of a charter school. These experiences were seminal.

"Some of the greatest companies like Dropbox or Facebook were all started by people under twenty-three years old at

21 Rogoway, Mike. 2018. "Fleet, 22-Year-Old Portlander's Startup, Raises Another $10 Million". *Oregonlive.com*

the time. Some people really have the drive to move things forward in a way that is unpredictable. I realized this, especially while working with homeschoolers. Those students proved to me time and time that things could be different. I treated these ten-year-olds like they are real human beings because it is really important to them. When they go about their projects, they're so matter-of-fact and they're thinking, 'Yeah I'm doing this thing and I need these resources.' They're completely serious. At 1517, we're not afraid of youthfulness."

Ah, here's an idea. Maybe the success of a company is not tied to the titles a founder has held as much as the value the founder can bring and is willing to create. This is something Strachman has realized throughout her career in education without a single degree in that field. Just as much as 1517 is taking a chance investing in young entrepreneurs, the world has given Strachman a chance to prove herself as a principal with no experience just the same. Perhaps there's almost an advantage with inexperience.

"I'm used to backing people without a tracked institution. I don't even have a degree in education and the people I work with have no degree in finance—yet I've been able to work in [venture capital] and I've been in alternative education for fifteen years. I started tutoring companies for homeschooled kids. Then started I a charter school with no experience. It was me and a homeschool mom I knew from my tutoring

company and we were thinking let's start a charter school…
I had never run an organization much less started a school
before. The beauty of being young is that you don't know what
the problems are in the space you're working in so you're
willing to endure.

"If people asked me if I would start another school I would
say maybe, but mostly no because now I know the pain and
suffering associated with it. Sometimes the ignorance of how
hard something is helps people understand the backlash.
People think that to have the necessary experience you have
to be employed by somebody else. What we're finding is that
there's a ton of people at a young age with experience. They've
been learning to code, doing robotics, competing at things,
etc. Twenty years ago you'd find a small handful of people
who would know what coding was whereas now there are
people who have been coding from eight years old. That's a
great advantage."

Strachman has had more than enough experience to convince herself that "young" does not mean "inferior." However, the real catalyst that convinced her to create her fund
was after she joined as a program director on the founding
team of the Thiel Fellowship.

It is no secret that gifted students at talented high schools
decide to make an educational use out of their summers

through enrichment camps, leadership programs and the like. As a high school student in the Bay Area, I had some friends who had participated in something called the Thiel Fellowship. Specifically focused on young entrepreneurs, the Thiel Fellowship gives away $100,000 every year to the crème de la crème of those under twenty-two.22 Needless to say, the friends I knew who participated were extraordinarily impressive. Little did I know that the Thiel Fellowship is Strachman's brainchild.

"It is like an older person's homeschool program, like an independent study. People laugh but learning by doing is one of the best ways to learn for some people. Some people are book people. Some people are doers. At 1517, we do these $1,000 grants—about twenty a year—no equity or anything and we Venmo the payment. People like that. They're hard at work and don't want something that feels school-y.

"We noticed that thirty-six companies out of the five batches accepted in our programs went on to become actual companies or nonprofits. Of those thirty-six, seven of those companies moved toward series A and beyond. I was on the founding team with a lot of my colleagues and 1517 started because we noticed something. Hey maybe there's a thesis

---

22 Foundation, The. 2018. "The Thiel Fellowship". The Thiel Fellowship.

here for a VC fund for high school dropouts, and we saw a market for that. It just turns out that eight of our portfolio companies have been grantees, but we never intended it to be that way. We thought it was goodwill and rapport building with young people but they came back with great ideas. We've read over ten thousand apps, so when someone sticks out, we look at each other and we're thinking that this person reminds us of this founder or that one.

"We use sports analogies, so it is much like a batter has taken many swings and some turn into home runs—with young people, some of their projects turn into companies or nonprofits. Michael and I wanted to go big or go home with our work and we thought of what we could do. There was something there. We saw young entrepreneurship not as a fad but as a trend over time. Similarly, we have thirty investors ourselves and we haven't been in finance. We haven't run a VC fund before. We have a novel thesis and we know where to find these people. Again this sporting analogy—we want to see early players on the field and meet people and keep in touch with them over time, and we have systems to stay organized and so when these young entrepreneurs grow we will be there in time."

The ability to access promising deals otherwise overlooked by investors is a competitive asset for a venture capitalist like Strachman.

"I was talking to someone at a women-in-investing lunch and she asked if there were any interesting deals she should get on. I said she should look at this team that is working with some interesting data. She really appreciated it and said, 'I feel bad. You always have a deal for me but I don't ever have one for you because when I talk to entrepreneurs I always ask, 'Do you have experience?' and usually, when you're twenty you don't.'

"I talked to a young woman yesterday and she told me, 'Thanks for taking this meeting in person. Most people I talk to in the bay area, and I live here, start with a phone call.' A lot of people think they can sacrifice quality for efficiency and they miss out on a lot of things because they're not willing to talk to people early. We are the only fund that specifically targets dropouts. No one really does that. Most people don't have that stomach to go out for people who have dropped out, but we think that's actually such a valuable quality. They're willing to buck an entire social system for their business. It's one thing to be out of school and try this start-up and another to say, 'Hey, Mom and Dad and friends, I'm going to go do this...' That's a totally different level of commitment. When people are willing to leave the expectations placed upon them, that shows real devotion and endurance."

Strachman has had the benefit of more than a decade-long career in education to understand the potential of young people but what of her limited partnerships? But how do you get your limited partnerships on board to spend millions on teenagers and young adults?

"We showed people the hypothetical track record. We showed them the companies at the Thiel Fellowship and what would have happened if we had invested in the Thiel Fellow partnerships as VCs and not as grants, and we look at what outcomes we would have had. Our LPs agreed, people should be capitalizing on that and they work with us because we know how to spot them and mentor them."

Strachman knows to talk to, not talk down to, the young entrepreneurs she works with—a leading principle at 1517. Strachman isn't just your VC. She's your advisor, your mentor, a sounding board and she gives you the ultimate sign of respect no matter how old you are—she's honest with you.

"Back in the early days before the fund, we followed up with those $1,000 grantees to see what they were up to. For Max, who ended up pitching to Start-up Battlefield at TechCrunch Disrupt, it wasn't about the money. He said more than the $1,000 grant, what really mattered was that real people in Silicon Valley believe in his idea. 'You believed in me first.' People say that time and time again. People constantly come back to us and say that.

"If VCs don't want to make an investment decision, they think, 'This space isn't for us. We'll look later.' That's not how you build relationships. We're really frank with people: 'This is great. You should be doing it and there's a market, but it is just unclear to me if this is a venture scalable business.' When people raise money, people know we're a safe firm to work with. What safe means is that we give them feedback. It is all an opportunity.

"I see all of these things as a learning opportunity. That's one thing we look for. When talking to founders, are they listening and having thoughtful conversations? We ask: 'What have you learned recently? Because I want to learn alongside you.' Reality is the best teacher. We're just here to talk about things you've learned. Part of the VC ride is having faith that we're in this business together. Our goal is to find a really great founder or founders who will build a great team and work together."

ANN WEISS: MAESTRO OF THE MOM MARKET

To my surprise, the road to venture capital is anything but streamlined. I embarked on this journey thinking that to get to partner-level positions, working in finance or consulting for a few years before business school was in order. It turns out many of the women I talked to have shared that their life experience is in starting their own company.

I was very lucky that one person in my Undergraduate Venture Capital Investment Competition (UVCIC) group had worked for the illustrious Ann Weiss over the summer at True Ventures. Not only did we consult her for invaluable advice on our competition, but we also brought her to Georgetown to hold an information session on working in venture capital and entrepreneurship—something she's had two start-ups worth of experience on.

It is fitting that Ann is a venture partner at a place called True Ventures because Ann truly wants to be every new parent's trusted partner. True partnership is a mantra that both True Ventures and Ann embody. For Ann, this idea of being a new parent's trusted partner manifests in her start-up Hatch Baby.

"I am a mom of three kids and I know. Having been through this journey now for fifteen years—how difficult it is and how much external support you need—that's the fundamental belief that keeps me going. Hatch Baby is designed to be a support for moms and dads, and I believe in my heart of hearts that it is meant to be. A brand will dominate this space. It is a core human need to feel supported as a new parent and that's why I'm here. I can personally relate and I know it is a very significant business opportunity. These are both hyper-motivating to me."

Ann's dedication to parents isn't just born out of her own experience as a mother of three, but also as an entrepreneur passionate about creating a better connection with customers. After her last exit with Maya's Mom, Ann realized there should be no compromise to deliver the best product experience to consumers.

"My first start-up was entirely software based. It was back in 2006 and at the time MySpace was all the rage, and Facebook was not yet opened. We created a verticalized version of MySpace that was designed for parents. It was awesome and we were super fortunate to have a great exit. The thing I wanted to do differently though in my second is that I really wanted to produce something people paid for. I wanted something people took out their credit cards and paid for because Baby Center and Mayas Mom were entirely ad-supported. And the challenge with something that is ad-supported is that you have two masters. You have the advertiser as your master but you also have the consumer—the person whose eyeballs you're trying to gain as your master. I really did not like that. I really felt like we compromised a lot about the product experience to please advertisers, and ultimately that is not a formula for success. I wanted to make sure Hatch Baby was very much focused on the human beings that were going to consume the actual product and not on a third party that wanted to somehow influence human beings."

True Ventures took Ann—an operating CEO of a portfolio company—as a venture partner because she could contribute her experience as a successful founder to the partnerships with True's portfolio companies.

"For us, a venture partner is that I'm an operating CEO of a portfolio company. So I run a company called Hatch Baby that True is an investor in. That's how I spend most of my time—as an operating CEO. We have another venture partner named Amy Errett, who is also on the True Ventures team. She's an operating CEO and also an investor. For us, that's what a venture partner means.

"We are an operating CEO in addition to being venture capitalists at True Ventures. I think it is fairly unique. Being a venture partner is not unique but being an operating CEO and an investor is a fairly unique thing to do. We do it because it works. We do it because we, as operating CEOs, see things you don't see if you just work in traditional venture capital. I see latest trends in marketing. I see how to use social media. We bring a different perspective to team discussions when we're looking at things. We can say, 'I've used that and I think it really works.' Or, 'I've used a different product and I think we should look at this.' We just have firsthand experience that really complements the experience of the rest of our team."

That firsthand experience is something pretty unique. Not everyone has the guts to pursue creating their own company, as there are significant financial, emotional, and lifestyle risks with creating your own company. The emotional hardiness Ann has had to build through two start-ups helps her better understand whether an entrepreneur pitching to True Ventures has what it takes to return the fund.

"Hatch Baby is my second venture-funded company. The reality is, it is hard. I think there are probably zero founders who have gone through this journey without great difficulty. The path to success is nonlinear. It is very up and down and sometimes backward and forward. There's no question that we've faced those things. One of those things for Hatch Baby was that we didn't know anything about creating hardware devices. I knew the mom market really, really well. That was my first company. I was in the same mom-market, and I ran a company called Baby Center, which is the single largest place for new and expecting moms to get information, but I did not know anything about hardware.

"At Hatch Baby we started out creating hardware devices and it was really hard. We definitely made mistakes along the way and it is not easy to have something like it. The first beta device we put out had problems with the first two hundred units, and it was a huge deal. We had sleepless nights for many nights. So there are lots of things that can go wrong.

That's one example. There are many of them. You have to believe in your soul that this is worth pursuing because there are a lot of scary things along the way and can shake you to your core."

Imagine putting your savings, reputation, and emotional energy on the line for years with no clear outcome for success. Are you sweating yet? Okay now imagine you're also pregnant while doing that. Now do that twice. Most people quake at the idea. For Ann starting a company as she grew her family was a golden opportunity.

"Some people know they were meant to be stay-at-home moms, and some people don't have a choice, but I was lucky enough to have a choice. And I knew to be a happy mom, work was the right thing for me to do. But, I also knew I wanted to do something that was very meaningful for me. Working for someone else on an idea at a company that was really just a job was not what I wanted to do. The reason having kids made entrepreneurship so attractive is because it was so meaningful to me. Going to work is fun for me. If I'm going to be away from my kids, which again I know is the right thing for me, I want to be doing something that I'm super passionate about."

Beyond embarking on a meaningful journey, Ann is also amongst the sliver of people who get to experience the joys of a successful company. Finally, after starting Hatch Baby, Ann got to experience that connection with customers through the product she was seeking after her first venture. Her ability to understand her customer segment to such an intimate degree led to her product, Rest, selling out on Amazon almost immediately each time Hatch Baby restocks.

"I had my very first time that a random person posted on Facebook about using Rest. It was super exciting. Basically, she was writing on one of our ads. She wrote to one of her friends to say, 'I used this and it changed my life and we are now sleeping in our house!' Sleep is a huge thing for families. It is such a lovely thing. And now we see it all the time. Now we're on Amazon and I get to read the reviews, and it is really so meaningful as a founder. I had no idea as an individual that when I wrote a review or when I wrote a comment that anyone would read it. You just don't think about the humans behind the product and it was thrilling.

"By the way, the opposite is also true. With our product sometimes it is really devastating to know that something crapped out on them and those things are really tough. Whenever we read those, we respond to them and say, 'Contact us and our customer support will give you a new one!' But people don't necessarily think of that and sometimes they write a review and you can't even get in touch with them anymore."

Throughout this journey of starting two companies, Ann knows what resilience and grit look like. This intimate understanding of the realities of the entrepreneurial experience, while also appreciating its joys, prepares Ann to evaluate founders like her. Will they understand what kind of support True Ventures can provide them? Are they the kind of people who will see the success of their product to the end, no matter what the obstacle?

"We do a lot of referencing of our founders to make sure they have the right experience and have the right profile of emotional fortitude and stick-with-it-ness to make it happen. The reality is everyone goes through good and bad times, and we want to make sure everyone we're working with is resilient and will keep on going even when times are tough."

Hiring qualified and experienced professionals like Ann is not the only way True Ventures has solidified its mantra of meaningful partnership. At True Ventures, no one leads a deal. Instead, everyone leads all the deals that True invests in.

"It is unique. We don't have what's called attribution. If you look at our website there's not this person did this deal this person did this deal. We don't publicize that at all because we believe the entire firm should take ownership of all the investment decisions we make. The reason for that is that we want to be a true partnership. We want to be a collaborative organization that roots for each other and in traditional venture capital that's not the case. In traditional venture capital, you make money on the deals that you do primarily and we want to be a true partnership where we all are on the same team rooting for the overall success of the business."

ACTION ITEMS AND EXERCISES

PICK YOUR SPECIALTY

What are you an expert at? It doesn't have to be venture capital. Just as Danielle and Ann came into venture capital with the expertise of an educator and a mother, you've got some unique angle too! Write your passions down on a list and think about how you could use your knowledge in those fields to start a business. Look into start-ups within that interest. What makes them interesting or unique? Be able to talk about these in conversation, lest you ever run into a VC and have the chance to make a lasting impression about your expertise in a certain sector.

FIND AN ADVOCATE

Just like how Danielle is an advocate for the young adults that come through her fund, find someone who you can bounce ideas off of. Perhaps that would be a professor or a mentor who can offer impartial advice.

PART II

WHERE WE'RE GOING

CHAPTER 8

SUPPORTING FEMALE INVESTORS ALSO MEANS SUPPORTING FEMALE FOUNDERS.

———

You don't have a unicorn founder without a VC, and you don't have a VC without any founders. When it comes to a discussion on gender diversity in venture capital, that also indirectly means a conversation about diversity in entrepreneurship.

A common reason male allies push for more women in venture capital is that women have a lens of understanding for sectors men don't usually look at. I have some qualms about this viewpoint as it also is stereotyping and assigning gender roles to entrepreneurship, but the consumer and retail space is one women have become high-performing leaders in as retail is an industry more women are knowledgeable in. Women account for 85 percent of all consumer purchases23 and so a female investor is much more likely to understand start-ups in this space. Kirsten Green and Eurie Kim's wild success with Forerunner Ventures investing in the consumer space is a testament to that idea.

When I was getting a better feel for what the mosaic of firms and individuals in the investing space looked like, I spoke with Amy Millman from Springboard Enterprises. Amy Millman had worked in government committees studying entrepreneurship and the representation of women in them. Amy then went on to take her findings and create what is called an investment catalyst. She helps venture capital funding find companies led by women to invest in.

Amy told me it wasn't that there were no women entrepreneurs back in the day. It was more like women started companies that were not popular with venture capital funds. Women started lifestyle brands, consumer-facing products, and retail companies while venture capital at the time was busy investing in "boxier" products like hardware and

---

23 "The Purchasing Power Of Women: Statistics | Girlpower Marketing". 2018. *Girlpower Marketing.*

software sold in the enterprise space. However, now that the trends in investing have shifted toward consumer-facing products, you see "more" women in entrepreneurship being represented than before. To illustrate, Amy told me about the story of Julie Wainwright the CEO of TheRealReal.

Though TheRealReal was founded in 2011, Julie was way ahead of her time. She is known for her huge success with TheRealReal, but her company Pets.com was one of the victims of the 2000 dot-com crash. 24At that time there was no market, no infrastructure for e-commerce the way we do now. Back then no one really did online shopping but now eight in 10 Americans are now shopping online.25

While it is a strength that women absolutely excel in these fields, it is also important to create equity in male-dominated entrepreneurship categories too. Just as how we strive to encourage women to join STEM fields, we should encourage them to create STEM-centered businesses. Women need to have a voice at every table, especially the ones leading change in the technologies that will change everyone's lives.

---

24 Mac, Ryan. 2018. "From Doghouse To Penthouse: The Remarkable Recovery Of The Realreal's Julie Wainwright". Forbes. Accessed October 19 2018. https://www.forbes.com/sites/ryanmac/2015/09/09/the-realreal-pets-julie-wainwright-doghouse-to-penthouse/.

25 Perez, Sarah. 2018. "79 Percent Of Americans Now Shop Online, But It'S Cost More Than Convenience That Sways Them". Techcrunch.

Ann Miura-Ko agrees with that, "We need more women starting companies that are not necessarily gendered. So, not approaching a gendered product for females. We need more generalized consumer applications and enterprise software founded by women. We need women who are involved in watching start-ups."

If women investors care about leveling the playing field to support women and crack the glass ceiling, they've also got to be keen on helping women own their start-up idea and help female founders understand the ins and outs of funding. Jenny Lefcourt, a two-time successful founder-turned-investor, is dedicating her time to just that. As a partner at Freestyle Ventures and a successful entrepreneur, she's an expert at cracking wider the 2 percent margin of VC funding that have been spent on women founders. She's working to put power in the hands of founders to influence investments for minority leaders.

JENNY LEFCOURT: FROM ONE FEMALE FOUNDER TO ANOTHER

I always get a little bit nervous the day of a call with a VC. Who wouldn't? These are influential professionals who have the power to move millions with a stroke of their pen. I was particularly nervous to talk to Jenny Lefcourt. The Wharton and Stanford Business School grad started and exited Weddingchannel.com to The Knot for $90M in 2006. Since then she's invested in and consulted for top entrepreneurs and companies including Minted, StyleSeat, lover.ly, MainStreetHub, WeddingtonWay, and others before becoming a partner at Freestyle, raised a total of $230.2M across 5 funds.

That morning I took a look at her twitter to catch up on what was new with her. Expecting to see tweets about news on portfolio companies like the other investors I've interviewed, I instead found Brian Chesky (CEO of Airbnb), Logan Green (CEO of Lyft), Kevin Systrom and Mike Krieger (founders of Instagram) holding up the words "We are founders for change." There were at least twenty photos posted of famous founders posing with the slogan.

The questions I had planned for our conversations immediately changed. This movement of over seven hundred-plus influential founders is asking for diversity in their funding source. Why did Jenny Lefcourt participate in creating this organization?

"Founders for Change is not about [VCs], it is about founders announcing that they did something that supports this yesterday, or now they see the light and in their next round they're going to do things differently."

There is undoubtedly an increase in the dialogue on diversity in the entrepreneurship and venture capital space. Founders for Change is an association of founders who care deeply about diversity and have been educated about the importance of diversity and its correlation to company performance. The majority of the founders—at least the ones Jenny has spoken with—are working hard on diversity and inclusion within their organizations.

"Now taking this to the next level, a lot of [founders] don't just care about diversity within their organizations but understand the importance of diversity at the board level and then also diversity on their cap table."

For this new wave of founders, diversity will be a point of consideration when choosing which venture capitalist to work with when they raise their next round of funding. This concerns diversity at the highest ranks—not just the executive assistants or the support staff.

"I know five stories, she knows five stories, this may be interesting. The more we talked to founders, the more we found founders taking action based on it. And so we thought, 'Wow if the venture community knew about this new important consideration for founders, they would probably diversify faster. VCs used to have terms in their term sheets with companies and then founder friendliness terms became hot. Founders care very much not just about valuation but about those terms, and when the customer of the VC, otherwise known as the founder, cared about it, the VCs changed. We felt that illuminating this group of founders and collecting their voice could be really good for the ecosystem overall."

It is not like venture capital has to be diverse. Jenny's collaboration with Founders for Change puts diversification in a favorable light for venture capitalists on their own value systems.

"What I like about Founders for Change is that it puts it in their business interest to be diverse because founders care. If I were to stay competitive, I would definitely diversify. There was an article from *The New York Times* yesterday. One of the founders the reporter spoke with, Trevor, has VCs who want to fund his deal and he sent emails out to big firms like Andreessen saying, 'No I don't want to meet with you because you don't have diverse partners.' I think it is hopefully a bit of a wake-up call. Once again, if VCs recognize they need to diversify to stay competitive, they'll diversify. And when they diversify, other VCs will see a greater diversification and greater diversity in funding."

While Founders for Change has shown such positive support, working to increase diversity in a stubbornly homogeneous industry isn't always the most reaffirming pursuit.

One of Jenny's good friends is Joanne Wilson—an angel investor and co-founder of the Women's Entrepreneurship Festival at Gotham Gal Ventures. She's backed hundreds of really early entrepreneurs with a really diverse portfolio and has a reputation for supporting the portfolio companies she works with. Jenny sat in on one of Joanne's panels at the WEF and spoke about the chilling perspective some shared.

"[Joanne Wilson] supports her entrepreneurs like no other. She put on a women's entrepreneurial event a couple years ago and she had me on the panel with some awesome women. These women. The women in the audience looked like deer in headlights. One of them stood up at the end and said, "What do you recommend to women like us when we know the odds of us raising capital are slim to none."

Everyone in the space knows the data. Only two percent of venture dollars were allocated to women in 2017. It is so disheartening to begin any process believing it is not your reality. Taking on not just a start-up, but a venture-backable, start-up means that your business must be of such a scale that it requires millions of dollars of costs with the responsibility to multiply that into hundreds of millions for your investors. It is hard enough to convince people to give anyone that much money, but even harder when you know that only 2 percent of that hard-negotiated money is likely to ever be written for you. If you believe you're beginning on any journey knowing that the reality is against you, there is no positive imagery to lend you strength. Jenny breaks this concept down with an analogy we can all understand.

"My kid plays baseball and you're supposed to be able to visualize yourself hitting the home run as you get up to plate. It is proven to be correlated to success and lots of things. Hearing these women say the exact opposite at the beginning of the process means they already believe they're not going to be successful. I respected the fact that the media is out there and is all shining a light onto our terrible performance as it relates to diversity and the capital that gets to diverse people, but I also hated that the people out there believe the odds are against them because that is not going to help them at all."

This one applies not just to female venture capital investors, but also to female founders. It may be a very Lean In type lesson, but women tend not to outwardly portray their confidence the way men do. This disadvantages them from stepping up to grab the roles they want or, in the realm of entrepreneurship, the funding they need.

Kirsten Green explains, "In the venture ecosystem, we are looking to invest in these outsize investment opportunities, and I think a founder who tends to be successful in getting something off the ground is not afraid to own their idea. Their ambition displays real leadership and confidence and they're not afraid to ask for what they need and what they want. Maybe as women we haven't been doing enough of that, with real authority and conviction with what we're doing."

ACTION ITEMS AND EXERCISES

BE WELL-VERSED ON FOUNDERS' ISSUES

Just like how Jenny Lefcourt is taking into account the concerns of founders—be familiar with the other things founders care about. You'll inevitably have to work with them if you work in VC, so understand what kinds of issues matter. For example, how stake ownership can affect their ability to stay on the company after venture dollars.

An important factor for venture capital investors' success is their ability to source deals and maintain relationships with founders and potential start-up investments. If you can excel with founder relationships because you understand founders well, that gives you an inarguable advantage.

CHAPTER 9

RETHINK IMPACT, RETHINK INVESTING

———

"It will cost the women in this room more than a million dollars over the course of their lives. If you don't invest as much as men do, it can cost you a $100 a day over the next ten years."

When the former CEO of Citigroup's Smith Barney and president of Bank of America's Global Wealth and Investment Management division tells you something about financial performance, you better be listening. Especially when she tells you that, "Women study after study after study outperform men by a percentage point a year, which really adds up. That's mostly because we don't pay fees like guys do because we don't panic as much in downturns."

Sallie Krawcheck, cofounder and CEO of the investment platform for women called Ellevest, noticed during her career as the most senior woman in Wall Street that there was an incredible gender investing gap. "For some reason, Wall Street has blamed women [for the investing gap], claiming that they're risk averse, they need more financial education, they're not as good at investing, they're not good at math. That is not true. What we should have been saying is that we built a product for men because investors are mostly men [at 86 percent]."

As we cited last chapter, women are not incompetent. In fact, they are consistently outperforming financial expectations and now hold a majority of personal wealth in the US while also making a majority of buying decisions. If venture capitalists are looking ahead for investments to turn into hockey-stick successes, the future is indeed female.

According to a report from First Round Capital of their portfolio investments, portfolio companies with at least one female founder performed 63 percent better than companies with all-male founding teams.26 While female founders are more likely to give the outsized returns VCs are looking for, VC firms with female partners are more than twice as likely to invest in companies with a woman on the management team (34 percent of VC firms with a woman partner

---

26 "First Round 10 Year Project". 2018. *First Round 10 Year Project*.

versus 13 percent of VC firms without a woman partner).27 Women investing in other women is not just equitable, it is more lucrative.

Enter Jenny Abramson (@abramsonjenny), founder and managing partner of Rethink Impact (@rethinkimpact), a venture capital firm investing in female leaders using technology to solve the world's biggest problems, believes the next generation of extraordinary companies will find success through their relentless pursuit of mission for the benefit of all communities. Rethink Impact invests in gender-diverse teams using technology to tackle issues in health, education, environmental sustainability, and economic empowerment.

Many of the industries Jenny invests in are also ones she has worked in herself. Sound like a lot to handle? It is. Not only did she graduate with honors on her BA and MA from Stanford, she got the Dean's Award from Harvard Business School when she nabbed her MBA. Oh, did I mention she was a Fulbright Scholar focusing on Human Genomics at The London School of Economics? Casual.

She's led roles in education, personal data, tech, and media. She was the CEO of LiveSafe, a company that helps prevent school shootings and sexual assault. As an aside, LiveSafe, is

---

27 Stengel, Geri. 2018. "Women Get It Done: Fixing The Broken Venture Capital System". *Forbes.*

now used in over a hundred schools across the country and keeps students like me safe by crowdsourcing information and enabling quick, discreet communication with campus security. LiveSafe manages risk in workplaces too, making meaningful contributions to crime prevention tactics.

She held significant business leadership roles at *The Washington Post*, Personal (a data tech company), and The Boston Consulting Group. Even contributing to her community and country, Jenny also oversaw the Transformation Management Office for DC Public Schools Chancellor Rhee and served as the director of strategy and development at Teach for America. She's been featured at the United Nations, on Capitol Hill, and was a *Forbes'* Top 40 under 40.

Despite all these leadership roles, I think the part that impresses me the most is how down to earth Jenny is. When we began our call, we talked about how my book was going and how her niece is also likely to come to Georgetown next year. She shared how growing up with a mother who was also an investor helped shaped the way she began investing in women.

"Despite having worked with fabulous female peers throughout my career, when I was a tech CEO, I often noticed that I was the only female on a given stage or situation and was puzzled by why this was the case. I dug into the data and realized that when my mom, who had been investing in women twenty years ago, was investing women actually got a larger percentage of total venture capital dollars28 than they get today.29 This investment gap exists, despite the fact that there is all sorts of data showing that teams with gender-diverse leadership outperform.30 It, therefore, was logical to focus on investments in portfolio companies that coupled the gender market opportunity with the impact opportunity and invest in terrific female entrepreneurs leading businesses across our core verticals of health, education, environmental sustainability and economic empowerment."

When Jenny Abramson says there is data on the power of gender-diverse leadership teams, she isn't kidding. Here's a snapshot:

1) THE BUSINESS CAPABILITIES OF WOMEN:

Companies with a female founder performed 63 percent better than those with all-male founding teams.31 Though this is such a positive figure it might also come from a not so great reason.

---

28 The Diana Project. "Women Business Owners & Equity Capital: The Myths Dispelled." 2001

29 Fortune. "Female Founders Got 2 percent of Venture Capital Dollars in 2017." 2018

30 Peterson Institute for International Economics. "Firms with More Women in the C-Suite are More Profitable." 2016

31 Ibid.

Ann Weiss from True Ventures explains this phenomenon: "There are also different ways women and men present themselves. Google did some research, looking at their very best-performing engineers, and had them self-rate themselves. The very best male engineers rated themselves a 5/5 and the very best female engineers rated themselves 4/5. And they were such an equally competent group of engineers but it just shows you that women as a general rule self-report lower than men. And that is a barrier when it comes to pitching for money because the reality is that when people pitch for money, they are pitching their billion dollar businesses. They are certain of their outcome, and their confidence is really important in pitching. If women who are amazingly competent are self-rating themselves lower than their male counterparts, that's going to be a barrier to getting money."

Because of this insecurity, many women may feel more of a need to check and research their hypothesis before proclaiming that their business idea is a valid one.

"I've had women come to me with pitches that are way better researched, but when they present they use "oh just this oh just that" language. They're not as confident as men even if their idea and market research is better. When you're pitching, you have to believe in yourself and your product for the investor to have faith in you too," said Ann Weiss.

2) THE PURCHASING POWER OF WOMEN AS A TARGET SECTOR:

Women account for 70 to 80 percent of all consumer purchases.32 Women control 51% of personal wealth in the U.S. and, over the next 40 years, are expected to inherit 70% of the $41 trillion in intergenerational wealth transfers.33 Undeniably, women understand women better than men understand women. More women generating businesses means more businesses that understand the preferences and concerns of a large sector of consumers.

3) WOMEN INVEST THEIR MONEY BACK INTO THEIR FAMILIES:

When women work, they invest 90 percent of their income back into their families, compared with 35 percent for men.34

4) INFORMATIONAL DIVERSITY AS A POSITIVE FORCE:

As I mentioned earlier, businesses with at least one female founder perform better than those that are all male. But what

---

32 "The Purchasing Power Of Women: Statistics | Girlpower Marketing". 2018. Girlpower Marketing. https://girlpowermarketing.com/statistics-purchasing-power-women/.

33 Prudential. "A Total Market Approach: Winning with Women and Multicultural Consumers." 2015

34 "Press Release: Corporations, Ngos, And Foundations Announce 13 New Commitments To Empower Girls And Women At The Fifth Annual Meeting Of The Clinton Global Initiative". 2018. *Clinton Foundation.*

is it explicitly about adding women to the team that makes a business so much more successful?

Jenny Abramson says, "A number of studies show why having diverse leadership teams can yield better outcomes. One study found that informational diversity—the differences in knowledge bases and perspectives arising from education, experience, and expertise—is positively related to group performance, and the effect was more pronounced when tasks were complex.35 When you have diversity in the management team, it brings unique perspectives to the table that, ultimately, can lead to better business decisions. This isn't just about gender diversity. It's about all kinds of diversity."

Jenny also understands another often overlooked nuance when it comes to investing in female-led start-up companies: the difficulty of raising follow-on rounds.

An excerpt from a report compiled by Dana Olsen on Pitch-Book shows: "More VC-backed male-founded companies in *every single industry* received follow-on funding than female-founded companies.…Companies with all-male founders receive funding after their first round nearly 35 percent of the

---

35 Administrative Science Quarterly, "Why Differences Make a Difference: A Field Study of Diversity, Conflict, and Performance in Workgroups"

time. For companies with all female founders, that number is less than 2 percent."

"It may be shocking to learn that only 17 percent of tech companies get to a Series B,36 and for women-led companies, that figure is only 5 percent,37" said Jenny Abramson.

One thing I've found in my research is the impact a non-diverse leadership team at a VC firm can have on the types of entrepreneurs they fund. The gender makeup of VCs in older albeit more powerful firms is dismal (which can lead to less funding going to female founders) while micro VCs and firms that have been founded by women are more diverse. It's easier to create your own culture than it is to try to change an existing one. Does that mean that traditional VC is shot? Do we keep trying to fix an old but influential society? Is it realistic or meaningful to only have diversity in funds that aren't as well embedded in the markets?

"It's important to have equity at all levels of the VC ecosystem—from those leading the businesses that are being funded to those being hired and/or promoted within venture firms, and beyond. This is what will drive change," said Jenny Abramson.

---

36 Mattermark. "The Start-up Funding Graduation Rate Is Surprisingly Low." 2016
37 Techcrunch. "Female Founders: The State Of The Union." 2015

Naturally, increasing the diversity of partners at venture capital firms can directly translate to dollars invested in companies with diverse leadership teams. Just like how some companies are known for having a problematic company culture from the start, a company just becomes an inflated version of itself as it grows. If the culture is toxic to begin with, the culture won't just clean itself up. Like attracts like.

"It's important to not wait to add diversity. I think more and more people will realize that it's not just good for the world, but also smart business," said Jenny Abramson.

Jenny is optimistic that the ecosystem of women in investment positions is changing for the better. "When you consider the fact that two thirds of all wealth in the US will be controlled by women in 2030,38 we can expect the landscape of investing to change dramatically in the future."

Beyond all this data that the business of investing in female-run businesses is the future, it is also a dutiful one. Having a mother who was also an investor in female entrepreneurs made Jenny more aware of the importance of really stepping up and supporting women.

---

38 Prudential. "A Total Market Approach: Winning with Women and Multicultural Consumers." 2015

Jenny said, "Given the fact that women earn almost 60 percent of undergraduate degrees, 60 percent of all master's degrees,39 make up almost half of business school classes versus a quarter 20 years ago,40 and are starting businesses at twice the rate of men,41 it can be easy to forget the investing gap that exists for female entrepreneurs."

Beyond Jenny's focus on gender, she also focuses on impact. She comes to this with real operational experience as she was the CEO of an impact tech company, and experienced how impact can not only not hurt a business, but benefit it. "As CEO of an impact company, I saw firsthand how social impact can be good for business." With the experience of being a CEO of a tech-driven impact company, Jenny had the data and the experience to know what she was looking to invest in when she founded Rethink Impact.

Reflecting on her experiences as CEO and now as founder and managing partner of an impact venture capital firm with a dedicated gender lens, Jenny was reminded of a *New York Times* article in which Henry Paulson stated, six trillion dollars of commercial capital must be unleashed—every year for

---

39 Center for American Progress. "Fact Sheet: The Women's Leadership Gap." 2014
40 Harvard Business School. "HBS Cases: Women MBAs at Harvard Business School." 2013
41 American Express. "The 2014 State of Women-Owned Businesses Report." 2014

the next fifteen years—if we want to see real change around poverty alleviation, climate change, and social equality happen in our lifetime.42 In concluding our discussion, she stated, "I am thrilled to be in a position to make real change around these issues and gender equality more broadly."

ACTION ITEMS AND EXERCISES

IDENTIFY STARTUPS THAT REPRESENT SOCIAL IMPACT VALUES YOU CARE ABOUT

Make a short list of at least 5 startups whose mission you can really stand behind. Be able to explain why what the company does matters and is a good business opportunity in conversation. Having this arsenal of impassioned conversation topics will come in handy when participating in discussions about investment and networking.

---

42 New York Times. "How to Raise Trillions for Green Investments." 2016

CHAPTER 10

BEYOND VENTURE CAPITAL

———

Up to this point, we've been talking about the problems in venture capital and how to navigate them. Now that you're well informed on the nuances of the gender dynamics of venture capital, let me propose something a little wild to you.

What if the system is broken?

What if we just shouldn't be using venture capital structured investing as a form of investment anymore.

"Well that might be interesting" you're probably thinking, "but what is the alternative?"

A new form of investing, where you take a permanent stake in a company and aren't looking for the next exit, is being pioneered by one of the most badass women I know. Nathalie Molina Niño.

Nathalie argues that urging to put more women in investing roles is just trickledown economics. It doesn't work. Of all the investors I've talked to, I think she is most concerned with lifting the standards for all woman-kind. And she doesn't care about the gender makeup of the companies she invests in.

"I don't care about pink-washing and headlines."

NATHALIE MOLINA NIÑO: HEAD CHICA IN CHARGE

One of the women I look up to most is my high school summer program director.

But this is no ordinary summer program. Entrepreneurs-in-Training at Barnard College is no bullshit. As a high schooler I had the privilege of being coached by the most emphatic speech givers, captivating story tellers, dedicated entrepreneurs, and wise women. During those two weeks of my junior year high school summer, I met both peers and mentors that I had limitless respect for. We got to create our own start-ups under the lean start-up model, learn that we are "the source of our own supply," visited the Etsy and Hanky Panky HQs. All this was under the guidance of Nathalie Molina Niño. She created her own website development business when she was twenty then sold it and bought a house. At twenty.

A chief revenue officer at PowertoFly, an Interim CEO at Self Made, the cofounder of Entrepreneurs at Athena at Barnard College, and now the CEO and founder of BRAVA Investments. What more can I say? Nathalie is somebody I am so glad I can talk to about investing. You can imagine my surprise when Nathalie told me, "I'm not a big believer in VC and in pipelining more women into it."

She goes on to explain the inherent issue with pushing more women into an industry where they likely have to change who they are in order to succeed, "In the eighties they had assertiveness training for women. You know, shoulder pad and suits. [The training] was about how we don't have enough women in business. So the solution was: make women act and dress like men. I don't want to act any differently. There's all this perception that VC is the coolest thing in the world. No one is stepping back and saying, 'Maybe VCs and their structure and how they work is broken.'"

VC is broken in more than one way—beyond the fact that it is exclusive and homogeneously white and male. VCs ironically invest money into start-ups because of their perceived potential, yet also don't care that much if a start-up fails. VCs invest only a sliver of their money into each business within their well-diversified portfolio. If that money is lost, it's not the end of the world for them.

VC funds typically have a lifespan of five to ten years per fund—short term endeavors by design. Their end goal is to exit at all costs by the end of those five to ten years. Say a portfolio company with a charismatic leader and a promising future is propositioned with a merger by a larger company near the end of the VC fund's lifecycle. Likely, the VC will want the company to sell, even if that may stunt the company's growth, so that they can make a return and make their LPs happy.

"It's put money in—and Peter Thiel calls it spray and pray—a hundred companies when you expect ninety of them to go bankrupt, but in the remaining ten, there is a unicorn. I have a problem with that. I have a problem with a society that is okay with throwing away ninety percent of the businesses they invest in. For these investors, when [entrepreneurs] go bankrupt it's okay because most of these founders have trust funds or other safety nets. Your average person going bankrupt is a dangerous thing. That means they lost their nest and don't have a retirement fund and in some cases they're homeless. Yet people in VC treat this like it's okay. They expected this to happen."

From the perspective of an LP, this approach makes financial sense. Imagine you are a multi-millionaire. You are wealthy enough that after your retirement fund, after a cushy lifestyle, after setting aside money for your kids and their kids, after investing in something sure to return but slow like stocks and bonds, you have still millions left just sitting there to be taxed. You're not gonna toss it in the trash can! You're gonna toss it into venture capital, where you know you could lose it but with the chance that it comes back twenty times the amount you put in. Whether or not you get it back really won't upset the way you've already been living.

These are great incentives to participate with a low-touch for an investor, but not so for entrepreneurs. While one side of the equation might be apathetic, their involvement can spell complication and doom for entrepreneurs.

"If you're getting venture capital funding, you're saying it's okay that this system exists because it means someone believes in your company more than just you. But these investors will often end up with the right to fire you from your own company. An underlying reason we want women investors is that they invest in women more. I definitely want more women out there, but do I want more women to get venture capital funding?

"The solution to gender equity is more than getting women into venture capital. Do we want more women to take on capital from people who encourage them to sell or shut down their companies just because they didn't make the 10x returns they wanted? Do we really want to put women into that system? Entrepreneurs come to me and say, 'I'm trying to get venture capital.' This is great if you've thought it out, but have you ever thought about terms that are onerous? Even though I'm an investor I'm like, 'Think three times before you do this.' Just because your company is growing fast doesn't mean [venture capital funding] is right for you."

I've never been disillusioned so fast. And then Nathalie challenged a core assumption we make when we talk about venture capital. The lure of firms like Andreessen Horowitz and Sequoia Capital is undeniably sexy. When we hear about these firms, we think of big money—a huge number times returns and billions of dollars. But that's exactly the problem.

We think all venture capital is crazy successful but are only hearing about the same ten or so huge firms that have those returns and resources to keep themselves on top of the VC world. Deal flow, access to LPs, name-brand recognition, and trust amongst entrepreneurs are all benefits these large, older funds have to stay lucrative. This is not necessarily the truth for the majority of other VCs out there.

"Looking at actual data out of the thousands that are venture funds, those which are actually making money is a single digit percentage. Most VCs are not making money."

Nathalie explains why the structure of the origin of VC dollars makes it so amenable to risk and thus failure. "I didn't come up knowing anything about trust funds or anything about big capital sources. For me it's an interesting learning process. If you have a family trust of $100 million, you take 80 percent and put it in stable non-risky stuff. All it's making every year is a five percent increase over the long haul. It's slow and incremental. Then, they'll take a small sliver of their $100 million and put it into private equity and an even smaller sliver—$5 million or something—and put it in something like venture capital.

"This is a capital source they don't care if they lose. It's kind of like gambling, but they put it in there on the off chance they get a huge return. You hedge by putting a tiny sliver of wealth in there. There's not a single person who puts a ton of wealth in VC, not a single one. You have to think about it that way. People have come to equate investing with venture capital, but it's not all the same. I think of it like flipping houses.

"If you were an old-school developer in New York, you develop buildings and entire city blocks or you build malls. You're doing real estate. This has existed for forever and it is real estate. But because flipping houses has become super sexy and it's on TV, when someone says they're in real estate people think they're saying they flip houses. VC for me is the equivalent of flipping houses. It's smaller numbers, higher risks and it's been equated with all of investing but it's a teeny sliver of what investing actually is."

So if Nathalie dislikes venture capital, how does Brava work? I'm not sure I know a word for an investment fund that focuses on start-ups, has LPs, and is structured like a VC firm but somehow also.... isn't a VC firm?

"My form of investing is more in line with that of Warren Buffet's. He was once quoted answering 'forever': as his answer to a question about the ideal holding time for an investment. Warren Buffet doesn't make investments for the short term. He makes them with the intention of holding forever. If you own 30 percent of Coca-Cola, which is more or less printing money, why would you try to buy low sell high? Why would you sell it? If I do it this way, every year when they give dividends I'm making money. That's [BRAVA's] philosophy. Long before Trump was in the industry, there was this spray and pray model and I personally think it's harmful to society to build a model where it's okay that 90 percent of [investments] fail."

Spray and pray is not just a ruthless investment strategy, but also one that likely leads to exclusion when it comes to investments. Since it's all a numbers game anyway, firms likely expedite their due diligence through subconsciously prejudiced means and pattern-matching. No VC with a small, exclusive team of investors can reasonably go through deep, meaningful due diligence with every start-up that pitches to them. From a resource perspective, it just isn't possible.

"It is not that you look at a hundred companies in order to invest in one company. You only get to do real diligence on maybe ten to narrow it down to the one you want to invest in. That means for every hundred investments, you have to research a thousand companies. Imagine what kind of capital you need to do diligence to all these companies over the years. Imagine the staff. These VC firms don't have that. The research is limited. So they privately would rather invest in a match with previously successful investments, which is a white dude who went to Harvard and looks like Mark Zuckerberg. If you take this approach, you have an automatic 'in' because you look like the fund's old unicorns. This is pattern matching, which, in my view, is finding nothing innovative ever. It is not super thoughtful."

Part of why VCs can't be super thoughtful is the way they work. They're structured so that there is a 2 percent management fee and a 20 percent carry. That 2 percent fee is not much. You'll charge 2 percent of a $100-million-dollar fund so there are only $2 million worth of fees and that's your limit to staff. If they do discover a unicorn and they do sell, they're pocketing that 20 percent carry and not all of it is being invested back into the company.

What I learned from Nathalie is that even if your fund has a great thesis and mission, it is especially hard as an emerging manager to be recognized by significant backers (LPs). While they say they support emerging managers with missions and diversity, they also first and foremost have egregiously high financial barriers to entry. This is a problem many truly emerging managers, like Arlan Hamilton from Backstage Capital and Nathalie, have to deal with.

"Arlan Hamilton started with a little over $2 million. You do the math. There's a reason why she has a day job. You don't really get to be a full-time investor until you have $50 to $100M fund. It's a chicken or egg thing. The big sources of capital are pension plans and endowments. You wouldn't expect it but the biggest union is the teachers' union: CalPERS. They have an emerging manager program and it sounds awesome. They're sitting on billions of dollars and claim they're prioritizing investing in emerging managers—focused on first-time investors who are women and people of color, people like me and Arlan.

"They say they have an emerging managers program and they want to bring me in but requirement number one to qualify for their global emerging managers program is to have at least $100 million in your fund. When people like CalPERS and other large institutions call $100M funds emerging, I think that's a misnomer. How is this even a thing? I did some research on some people who are qualifying for these emerging manager programs. You've got two bros, two dudes who have managed funds as employees from the likes of Bridgewater and BlackRock.

"You know what? They will structure the fund exactly the same way as their fund at Bridgewater. They will do the exact same thing and do it at a new company and call it new. From day one they've got $100M— from previous LPs. So when emerging manager programs from large institutions are looking for emerging managers, that's what they're finding and they're able to mitigate their risk.

"They'll think they got some new blood that's also super trustworthy since a lot of other people trusted them before they came on board. This versus a Nathalie who has a first-time $50M fund and no preexisting track record. I can see how Nathalie would seem super risky. That's fundamentally the challenging thing all emerging managers have to go through. That's why there are so many women in Micro VC and Angel investing."

Nathalie told me about one of her friends, former exec at JP Morgan. She started doing angel investing on the side. She started investing in companies and grew to have a portfolio of twenty companies. Nathalie pointed out how she was turning into a super angel to which she replied that she loves it and hates going to work every day.

After twenty years at JP Morgan she finally left and was thinking about joining BRAVA. She is an interesting example because she didn't really need a salary. She can take a few years off and afford to play around with a new career direction. However, if you're not independently wealthy, and you're like Arlan who became homeless right before getting her first funding check, it's super hard. If Nathalie is looking to bring on a principal, she's probably going to have to find someone who is independently wealthy like her friend who is willing to take a smaller salary. Though personally if I could, I would love to work on Nathalie's thoughtful investing experiment. She's building trust and a relationship with her investors in an interesting way.

"I've been investing where I find an amazing deal and I create a syndicate of investors. I've been investing without a fund. You don't have to trust me to the tune of many, many millions of dollars into a first time fund. Just do this one deal. Are you interested? People love these investments and they're potentially lucrative.

"Now I'm like, 'Okay, folks, now that you know me, I'm raising a fifty-million-dollar fund." It's easier since I now have a little track record. I have a few years to hurry up and deploy my capital. The way that I'm raising fifty million is so that I'm deploying twenty-five million. It's super unique as I'm keeping another twenty-five million to follow on.

"Not everyone does that, but I do that because VCs are really short term. I want to have a long-term relationship so that next time if you meet all your milestones and your company is doing really well, I will be here to invest, to get you to you the next step. I can't be Warren Buffet but I can start getting close to that. My eventual goal is to have enough money permanently capitalized to not have LPs, but I'm not starting with three hundred million dollars like Warren did. I'm trying to get there—trying to show that I did well with my first fifty million and then go back out there and be able to go to the calPERS of the world and have them get us to that billion."

ACTION ITEMS AND EXERCISES

RETHINK VENTURE CAPITAL!

Give this exercise a try. Pretend you're the managing director of your own fund. Draft up a thesis and write a one-pager that explains what you would care about most when looking to invest in companies. How long do YOU want to invest in them for? What kind of companies do YOU care about? It's okay if it's not mainstream, or hasn't already been done. Maybe you'll come up with something even better like Nathalie. Defining your own reasoning for investing into companies helps give you better direction as to what kind of VC, or any investing entity, you want to look for and why.

CONCLUSION

———

Throughout the journey of writing this book I've had the pleasure of speaking with and learning from a plethora of women in this space. From Jenny Abramson's impact-focused gender lens fund in Washington, DC, to Eurie and Kirsten's e-commerce-focused fund in the valley, I'm grateful for the breadth of funds and women I've encountered. Just as I wanted to show you don't have to be a man to be in venture capital, so too could your fund be outside the valley or focused on something other than enterprise software. Prior to venture capital, you even could have been a charter school principal like Danielle Strachman at 1517, a mother and entrepreneur like Ann Weiss, a product manager like Vanessa Larco, or an operator and a risk taker like Stephanie Palmeri. These women in venture prove that you can be anything you want to be.

Even though these women I've interviewed are all inspiring in their own right, there are still more women whose stories have yet to be told and whose experience lend themselves to the mosaic of women in venture capital. There is so much to learn from diversity, whether that be from diverse ethnicities, genders, or professional backgrounds. By now you know that start-ups with at least one female on the founding team perform much better than companies without, that women reinvest back into their families and that they hold the majority of private wealth. Why should women be barred from entering venture capital, an industry where investors have a meaningful impact on the future of our economy?

There is still so much improvement left to make in this space. I only managed to cover the issue of women's representation in venture capital (and only shared the stories of a selection of women), yet women of color comprise an even smaller subset of representation in venture capital. Not to mention, non-gender-binary identifying individuals have seen even less discussion on their inclusion in this space.

This valley is not just comprised of VCs either. Gender disparities must be worked on from the standpoint of engineers and start-ups as well. Start-ups have the ability to shape a culture and proliferate it from the very beginning. Gender inequality in the Silicon Valley in tech and in start-ups is an even larger beast and covered by other books such as *Brotopia* by Emily Chang or *Lean In by* Sheryl Sandberg. It is important to note that everyone, not just VCs, wield the power to contribute to a heterogeneous society that cares about a fair opportunity for everyone to take a piece of the pie.

SO WHAT DOES ALL THIS INFORMATION ON WOMEN IN VENTURE CAPITAL LEAVE US WITH?

My hope is that by the end of this book you've learned that even though the system is mostly men and has had its share of discrimination, it is worth giving your best shot as the women in this book show it is possible. It just requires confidence in your unique skillset, clever self-branding, and intentional networking.

Each of the women mentioned has had a unique path to venture capital. Each person's value-add is their own way of evaluating a start-up. Some women in this book are uniquely qualified because they've worked in a start-up, like Stephanie Palmeri, and they know the operational stumbles that could be a red flag in a potential investment. Others like Eurie Kim and Kirsten Green know a market so well that they are well-versed in its trends and know where that industry's future is heading. Don't get me wrong, obviously many are also financial experts off of Wall Street or consultants, but the key to being qualified enough to work at a VC firm is being able to prove you have a way to effectively pick the winners from the losers. That could be with or without an engineering degree (achem Michael Moritz).

Do something that makes you stand out. It sounds obvious, but you need to develop a personal brand that conveys your dedication and commitment in more explicit ways than to impress recruiters at other jobs. Standing out when recruiting for, say, an engineering position might mean you contributed to an interesting open source project or you led a winning team during a hackathon. Catching people's attention in venture could mean something like moving across the country with your two suitcases like Stephanie Palmeri or slamming magazines on a table like Jess Lee when you need to get your point across about how lucrative Polyvore can be. You don't want to just be impressive on paper. You want to shock them so they can't forget you.

Network purposefully and be upfront when talking to people in venture—guy or girl or anything in between. Homophily is real so be cognizant of it. Be upfront with what you want because you *are* qualified. According to the data from a Hewlett Packard internal review, men apply for a job when they meet only 60 percent of the qualifications, but women apply only if they meet 100 percent of them. Men who have the ability to hire you don't know to hire you or know that you're the perfect candidate for the job unless they first know you exist. Elect to sit at the all-boys table, as Ann Miura-Ko suggested.

Hearing how this set of women with diverse backgrounds have entered into venture capital, I can't help but feel hopeful that every woman should have as much of a fighting shot. I hope we can start to change the course of rhetoric on this issue. Instead of emphasizing the problem, let's focus on putting the solution in action.

ACKNOWLEDGEMENTS

—

I had the privilege of interviewing many women within the venture capital and entrepreneurship space. Their lessons and conversations have shaped the book into the reality that it is now and have shown me how I can pave my own path towards venture capital. Here are the stars that have been part of my journey through this book:

Trae Vassallo (Cofounder and Managing Director of Defy VC)

Stephanie Palmeri (Partner at Uncork Capital)

Ann Mirua-Ko (Founding Partner at Floodgate Fund)

Eurie Kim and Kirsten Green(Founding Partners at Forerunner Ventures)

Vanessa Larco (Partner at New Enterprise Associates)

Danielle Strachman (General Partner at 1517 Fund)

Ann Weiss (Partner at True Ventures)

Jenny Lefcourt (Partner at Freestyle Ventures)

Jenny Abramson (Founder and Managing Partner at Rethink Impact)

Chelsea Morris (Associate at Rethink Impact)

Nathalie Molina Niño (CEO of Brava Investments and Author of Leapfrog: The New Revolution for Women Entrepreneurs)

Joelle Kayden (Founder and Managing Partner at Accolade Partners)

Amy Millman (President at Springboard Enterprises)

Julia Klein (Associate at Greenspring Enterprises)

Thank you, also, to Brian Bies and Eric Koester for pulling my manuscript together and giving me a voice in this space.

APPENDIX

———

3. Lowrey, Annie. 2018. "Ellen Pao And The Sexism You Can't Quite Prove". *Intelligencer.*

4. Zarya, Valentina. 2018. "Female Founders Got 2% of Venture Capital Dollars in 2017". *Fortune.*

5. Teare, Genè, and Ned Desmond. 2018. "Announcing The 2017 Update To The Crunchbase Women In Venture Report". *Techcrunch.*

6. Feld, Brad, and Jason Mendelson. 2016. Venture Deals. Hoboken, NJ: Wiley.

7. Kulwin, Noah. 2018. "Venerated VC Michael Moritz Opens Mouth, Inserts Foot On Question About Hiring Women". *Recode.*

8. "Women In STEM: 2017 Update". 2018. *Department Of Commerce.*

9. "Women In Science, Technology, Engineering, And Mathematics (STEM)". 2018. *Catalyst.*

10. Torres, Lisa, and Matt L. Huffman. 2002. "Social Networks And Job Search Outcomes Among Male And Female Professional, Technical, And Managerial Workers". *Sociological Focus* 35 (1): 25-42. doi:10.1080/00380237.2002.10571218.

11. Bearman, Asher. 2018. "How VC Funds Work - Expenses And Management Fees | The Venture Alley". The Venture Alley. https://www.theventurealley.com/2011/01/how-vc-funds-work-expenses-and-management-fees/.

12. Fogarty, Kevin. 2018. "Why Men Have Stronger Professional Networks Than Women". *Ladders.*

13. "Women In Science, Technology, Engineering, And Mathematics (STEM)". 2018. *Catalyst.*

14. Vassallo, Trae, Ellen Levy, Michelle Mandansky, Hillary Mickell, Bennett Porter, Monica Leas, and Julie Oberweis. 2018. "The Elephant In The Valley". *Elephantinthevalley.Com.*

15. "TEAM". 2018. *Accolade Partners.*

16. Chaykowski, Kathleen. 2018. "Meet The Top Women Investors On Midas In 2018". *Forbes.*

17. Loizos, Connie. 2018. "Floodgate Closes Sixth Fund With $131 Million". *Techcrunch.*

18. Draznin, Haley. 2018. "Venture Capitalist Kirsten Green: We Need More Women Founders". *CNNmoney.*

19. "Forerunner Ventures Fund Overview". 2018. *Crunchbase.*

20. "Green, Kirsten – Forerunner Ventures". 2018. *Forerunnerventures.Com.*

21. "Kirsten Green, Founder Of Forerunner Ventures, Explains How Retail Needs To Change | Code Commerce". 2018. *Youtube.*

22. "Thesis". 2018. 1517 Fund. Accessed October 19 2018. http://www.1517fund.com/thesis/.

23. Rogoway, Mike. 2018. "Fleet, 22-Year-Old Portlander's Startup, Raises Another $10 Million". *Oregonlive.Com.*

24. Foundation, The. 2018. "The Thiel Fellowship". The Thiel Fellowship.

25. "The Purchasing Power Of Women: Statistics | Girlpower Marketing". 2018. *Girlpower Marketing.*

26. Mac, Ryan. 2018. "From Doghouse To Penthouse: The Remarkable Recovery Of The Realreal's Julie Wainwright". Forbes. Accessed October 19 2018. https://www.forbes.com/sites/ryanmac/2015/09/09/the-realreal-pets-julie-wainwright-doghouse-to-penthouse/.

27. Perez, Sarah. 2018. "79 Percent Of Americans Now Shop Online, But It'S Cost More Than Convenience That Sways Them". *Techcrunch.*

28. "First Round 10 Year Project". 2018. *First Round 10 Year Project.*

29. Stengel, Geri. 2018. "Women Get It Done: Fixing The Broken Venture Capital System". *Forbes.*

30. The Diana Project. "Women Business Owners & Equity Capital: The Myths Dispelled." 2001

31. Fortune. "Female Founders Got 2 percent of Venture Capital Dollars in 2017." 2018

32. Peterson Institute for International Economics. "Firms with More Women in the C-Suite are More Profitable." 2016

33. Ibid.

34. "The Purchasing Power Of Women: Statistics | Girlpower Marketing". 2018. Girlpower Marketing. https://girlpowermarketing.com/statistics-purchasing-power-women/.

35. Prudential. "A Total Market Approach: Winning with Women and Multicultural Consumers." 2015

36. "Press Release: Corporations, Ngos, And Foundations Announce 13 New Commitments To Empower Girls And Women At The Fifth Annual Meeting Of The Clinton Global Initiative". 2018. *Clinton Foundation.*

37. Administrative Science Quarterly, "Why Differences Make a Difference: A Field Study of Diversity, Conflict, and Performance in Workgroups"

38. Mattermark. "The Start-up Funding Graduation Rate Is Surprisingly Low." 2016

39. Techcrunch. "Female Founders: The State Of The Union." 2015

40. Prudential. "A Total Market Approach: Winning with Women and Multicultural Consumers." 2015

41. Center for American Progress. "Fact Sheet: The Women's Leadership Gap." 2014

42. Harvard Business School. "HBS Cases: Women MBAs at Harvard Business School." 2013

43. American Express. "The 2014 State of Women-Owned Businesses Report." 2014

44. New York Times. "How to Raise Trillions for Green Investments." 2016

Made in the USA
Monee, IL
09 September 2020

41583666R00090